Making Good Teaching *Great*

Everyday Strategies for Teaching with Impact

Annette Breaux
Todd Whitaker

Eye On Education
6 Depot Way West, Suite 106
Larchmont, NY 10538
(914) 833–0551
(914) 833–0761 fax
www.eyeoneducation.com

Library of Congress Cataloging-in-Publication Data

Breaux, Annette L.
Making good teaching great! : everyday strategies for teaching with impact/
Annette Breaux and Todd Whitaker.
    p.   cm.
ISBN 978-1-59667-212-3
1. Effective teaching.
2. Classroom management.
I. Whitaker, Todd, 1959–
II. Title.
LB1025.3.B742 2012
371.102—dc23   2011048296

Sponsoring Editor: Robert Sickles
Production Editor: Lauren Beebe
Copyeditor: Adrienne Rebello
Designer and Compositor: Matthew Williams, click! Publishing Services
Cover Designer: Dave Strauss, 3FoldDesign

All poetry in this book is the original work of Annette Breaux.

10 9 8 7 6 5 4 3 2

Also Available from EYE ON EDUCATION

50 Ways to Improve Student Behavior:
Simple Solutions to Complex Challenges
Annette Breaux & Todd Whitaker

Study Guide: 50 Ways to Improve Student Behavior:
Simple Solutions to Complex Challenges
Annette Breaux & Todd Whitaker

Seven Simple Secrets:
What the BEST Teachers Know and Do!
Annette Breaux & Todd Whitaker

Study Guide: Seven Simple Secrets:
What the BEST Teachers Know and Do!
Annette Breaux, Todd Whitaker, & Nancy Satterfield

101 "Answers" for New Teachers and Their Mentors:
Effective Teaching Tips for Daily Classroom Use
(Second Edition)
Annette L. Breaux

What Great Teachers Do *Differently*:
Seventeen Things That Matter Most
(Second Edition)
Todd Whitaker

Study Guide: What Great Teachers Do *Differently*:
Seventeen Things That Matter Most
(Second Edition)
Todd Whitaker

REAL Teachers, REAL Challenges, REAL Solutions:
25 Ways to Handle the Challenges of the Classroom Effectively
Annette L. Breaux & Elizabeth Breaux

Teaching Matters:
Motivating and Inspiring Yourself
Todd Whitaker & Beth Whitaker

Dealing With Difficult Parents:
And With Parents In Difficult Situations
Todd Whitaker & Douglas J. Fiore

We dedicate this book to those dedicated individuals
who are helping to ensure a better tomorrow,
one child at a time—teachers, true heroes!

About the Authors

Annette Breaux is one of the most entertaining and informative authors and speakers in education today. She leaves her audiences with practical techniques to implement in their classrooms immediately. Administrators agree that they see results from teachers the next day.

A former classroom teacher, curriculum coordinator, and teacher induction coordinator, she is also the author of Louisiana FIRST, a statewide induction program for new teachers. Annette has coauthored a book with Dr. Harry Wong on new teacher induction.

Her other writings include *101 "Answers" for New Teachers and Their Mentors* (2nd edition); *REAL Teachers, REAL Challenges, REAL Solutions; Seven Simple Secrets: What the BEST Teachers Know and Do; 50 Ways to Improve Student Behavior: Simple Solutions to Complex Challenges*, and *101 Poems for Teachers*.

Teachers who have read Annette's writings or heard Annette speak agree that they come away with user-friendly information, heartfelt inspiration, and a much needed reminder that theirs is the most noble of all professions—teaching.

Recognized as a leading presenter in the field of education, **Dr. Todd Whitaker** has been fortunate to be able to blend his passion with his career. His message about the importance of teaching has resonated with hundreds of thousands of educators around the world. Todd is a professor of educational leadership at Indiana State University in Terre Haute, Indiana. He has pursued his love of education by researching and studying effective teachers and principals.

Early in his career, Todd taught mathematics and coached basketball in Missouri. He then served as a principal at the middle school, junior high, and high school levels. He was also a middle school coordinator in charge of staffing, curriculum, and technology for the opening of new middle schools.

One of the nation's leading authorities on staff motivation, teacher leadership, and principal effectiveness, Todd has written more than twenty books, including the second editions of *What Great Teachers Do* Differently and *What Great Principals Do* Differently. Other titles include *50 Ways to Improve Student Behavior, Teaching Matters, The Ball, 7 Simple Secrets, Motivating & Inspiring Teachers*, and *Dealing with Difficult Parents*.

Todd is married to Beth, also a former teacher and principal, who is a professor of Elementary Education at Indiana State University. They are the parents of Katherine, Madeline, and Harrison.

Foreword

Do you want what every great teacher wants? To make a difference in the life of every student you teach? To instill a thirst for knowledge that will enable each student to eventually become his or her own best teacher? If so, this book will prove very useful to you.

In our ongoing observations of and conversations with teachers, we continue to learn that great teachers strive for two common goals: (1) to become a little better at their craft every day, and (2) to avoid making the same mistakes twice. You see, even the greatest of teachers make mistakes. They just try not to repeat those mistakes. No great teacher has ever told us, "My goal is to be perfect and to know everything there is to know about teaching." That's because great teachers know that no one ever finishes learning to teach—EVER! But all great teachers strive to improve on a daily basis. They strive to take small steps, each day, toward improvement, not perfection.

Thus, our intent in writing this book is not to give you the *definitive* answers to making you the *perfect* teacher. Rather, we will share simple, daily activities that will help to improve your teaching and your students' learning.

> *Every day, we'll provide you with a way*
> *To improve your teaching and your students' learning*
> *To increase the likelihood of students' yearning*
> *For in looking back, all great teachers hope to have instilled*
> *An insatiable quest for knowledge, a hunger never filled*
> *In each and every student whom they have had the privilege to teach*
> *And thus the goal of all great teachers, we will help you to reach.*
> —Annette Breaux and Todd Whitaker

How to Use This Book

This book is designed to be read in small bites, one day at a time, every day of the school year. If you acquire a copy during the school year, begin reading wherever you'd like. If you're on the 30th day of school, you may wish to begin on Day 30. Or, you may choose to simply start from the beginning. Each day, we will provide you with a simple activity for the day. Every 20 days, we will provide you with a short survey to assess what has worked for you and why, along with what you intend to carry forward in your daily teaching. We suggest that, at the end of each day, you glance at the next day's activity because occasionally you may want to prepare for the next day's activity a day in advance.

We are realistic enough to know that, due to the many demands placed upon you and the many unpredictable occurrences in your classroom, there may be days when you simply don't have the time to participate in the daily activity. It's your call, as you are the professional. If you have only sixty minutes with your students, and one of the activities that we suggest will take too much time away from your teaching on that particular day, then either don't do it or spread it out over several days or save it for a day when you have more time. Use your professional judgment, and always do what's best for your students on any given day. Your goal should not be simply to "cover" or "complete" this book. It should be to use this book as a tool for improving your effectiveness.

We hope that you will find, within these pages, many ideas that will help you improve teaching and learning in your classroom and that will help you to better establish what all great teachers enjoy—that oh-so-important positive rapport with students. With so many requirements placed upon us, as teachers, it is often easy to lose sight of the fact that though the content we teach is very important, students won't care how much we know until they know how much we care. The relationships we establish with our students will help to determine how much content they will or won't learn while they are in our care.

We believe that inside of every teacher lies an even better teacher waiting to emerge. We also believe that limitless possibilities lie waiting to be unleashed inside of every student. Through this book, we hope to help you to find your greater teacher, enabling you to help your students find their greater selves. Enjoy!

Contents

First Impression: Positive Expression

Think About It

A positive expression makes for the kind of first impression
That students will respond to in a positive way
So please ensure, please ensure that you're
Wearing a positive expression today!

Do It

Oftentimes, new teachers receive advice from other teachers that sounds like this: "Whatever you do, do not smile until Christmas!" or "Be mean until Halloween!" We wholeheartedly disagree with this type of advice. First impressions bear tremendous weight. They cannot be undone. If students walk into a teacher's classroom and see a serious, angry-looking teacher, they immediately become skeptical, guarded, and leery of the idea of ever trusting this teacher. And even if the teacher eventually "backs off" of this type of behavior, it is much more difficult to undo what has been done than it is to simply ensure a positive start from day one. Worse yet, if the teacher continues this "serious" approach with the students, it will be a long, difficult school year. The fact is that students need happy adults who serve as positive role models in their lives. You cannot help your students by being yet another negative influence in their lives. Therefore, it is vitally important that the first impression your students form of you is a positive one.

Today's activity is simple: Make a special effort to create a positive first impression on your students. The first and most important way to do that is to greet them with a smile. Since they are wondering what this year has in store for them in your classroom, be sure to tell them how excited you are to be teaching them and assure them that this will be a wonderfully successful year for the class. Tell of a few exciting activities you will be doing with them this year, and act as enthusiastic as possible. When they hear and see that you are happy and pleasant, they will be happier and more pleasant. It's a win–win!

Done!

Your first impression on anyone becomes a lasting one. Today, you have ensured that your students went home with a positive impression of you. This bodes well for tomorrow and for the rest of the school year. Now remember that they are expecting the same positive teacher to show up tomorrow!

DAY 2

Think About It

Some students sit in a place that is simply not conducive
To fostering good behavior. That's fact. It's conclusive!

Do It

If two students who lean toward inappropriate behavior are seated together, chances are good that behavior problems will ensue. We've found that great teachers don't share one common way of arranging seating, but they all have clever ways of doing so. Some allow students to sit where they choose at first. This allows teachers to get to know the students and better determine proper seating arrangements. They tell students to sit where they would like. Then they say something like, "I'll be changing the seating in a few days and possibly every few weeks for cooperative grouping purposes or so that I can see everyone better or for other reasons so that the classroom is conducive to optimal learning!" Then, when they see a need, they make a seating change. However, this is done with subtlety. If two students are misbehaving, the teacher doesn't stop and say, "Let's change your seats." That would be much too obvious. Also, effective teachers often change several seats at a time, and they always have a good reason for doing so. It's called clever psychology!

You may ask, "Why can't I let the students know that because they are misbehaving, their seats will be moved?" The simple answer is, "You can." However, you have just ensured that those students will misbehave wherever you seat them. Not a good outcome. Though we don't advocate ignoring all misbehavior, we do advocate picking your battles carefully. And we believe that battles over where the students sit can be avoided if handled appropriately by the teacher.

So your simple activity for today is to decide on a clever way to change student seating whenever the need arises without letting the students know you are trying to avoid behavior problems.

Done!

Feel free to use the method we've shared, come up with your own, or ask a fellow effective teacher for a clever idea for seating arrangements. Whatever method you choose, just remember to avoid making a seating change appear to be a punishment. And always make a seating change with a smile on your face!

I Really DO Want to Know About YOU

Think About It

Teachers who know their students well
Enjoy better behavior from bell to bell!

Do It

One of the best ways of getting the best from students is getting to know them on a personal level—learning something about who they are, what they believe, what their dreams entail, what they like and dislike, etc. And one of the best ways to initiate getting to know your students is by giving them some type of interest inventory. You can use one of the many existing ones or create your own. We suggest using a simple one consisting of only a few questions asking students to tell you about themselves. Some have open-ended questions such as "I am _____," " I like _____," "I don't like _____," "I enjoy _____," "I wish _____," "I hope _____," "I dream about _____." Students tell a lot about themselves in such activities, and you learn things you may have never learned otherwise that you can now use to better reach and teach each student. Therefore, your simple activity is to give your students some type of age-appropriate interest inventory. For very young children, the inventory may consist of having them draw a picture or two about themselves that they then interpret for you.

By giving your students an interest inventory, you have accomplished nothing less than the following: (1) You have learned something about each student, and (2) You have shown your students that you are interested in them as individuals. Don't ever underestimate the power of such an activity, regardless of age level or subject matter. All great teachers strive to connect with their students and understand as much as they can about each.

Done!

After giving your students some type of interest inventory, don't just file those away. If a student mentioned a special talent, begin conversing with the student about that talent. If you pick up on something that is really bothering a student, offer your support. USE the information in these inventories to help you better serve your students.

Some teachers post the results of the inventories in their classrooms, but only after securing permission from the students. Students are people, and every person has a story. Let them tell their stories!

DAY 3

DAY 4

Think About It

When parents feel welcomed and know you're not someone to fear
At concerts, meetings, and other school functions, they're more likely to appear!

Do It

We will not argue that it is often difficult to get some parents to attend school functions. We WILL tell you, however, that great teachers never give up on trying to involve parents in the education of their children. One of the ways they do this is by making a special effort to make parents feel welcomed, wanted, and valued.

A particular high school always had low attendance for back-to-school night. The teachers argued that it should be cancelled. The new principal refused to buy into the philosophy that parents of high school students won't attend school functions. He reminded the teachers that at sporting events, the stadium and gym were always filled with parents. Therefore, they decided to try an experiment. Instead of sending out the typical memo reminding parents of back-to-school night, each teacher made a phone call to his or her homeroom students' parents. The call sounded like this, even if leaving a message: "Hi, this is Ms. Simms, Ashley's teacher. I wanted to thank you for allowing Ashley to be in my class. It's a pleasure to teach her. I also wanted to personally invite you to attend our back-to-school night so that I'll have the privilege of meeting you. It's next Wednesday at 6 p.m. We'll treat you to some great refreshments. Hope to see you there!" So many parents attended that they had to bring in additional seating!

Try this with your own back-to-school night. Convince parents that you feel privileged to teach their children, and make every effort to help them feel welcomed in your school and in your classroom. Consider the fact that even for those parents who do not attend the function after receiving your phone call, you have still initiated positive contact. This will increase the chances that they will be more open to working cooperatively with you in the future.

Done!

We often receive feedback from teachers who are amazed at what a difference these simple phone calls make. Not surprisingly, we never hear of anything negative coming out of this activity. All great teachers make various attempts to involve parents. They know they have nothing to lose and only parental support to gain!

Classroom Management, Part 1

Think About It

Since to teach a student anything, you must first establish control
Then devising an effective management plan is a most important goal!

Do It

Classroom management. What is it? Is it the same as discipline? Not exactly. Discipline is one important piece of classroom management. An effective management plan involves everything the teacher does to ensure that the classroom runs smoothly and efficiently, to the point of appearing effortless. Appearing effortless, of course, is an illusion!

All great teachers are effective classroom managers. They put lots of thought and effort into how they arrange the desks, set structured rules and procedures, plan effective lessons, pace activities, manage time, and so on. They know that no matter how well they know their content, they can't teach any of that content until they can manage their classrooms. They know that without management, discipline problems arise and student achievement suffers. When a teacher is disorganized, the students follow suit. When a teacher is inconsistent with following through on consequences when students break rules, the students are inconsistent in obeying the rules. If a teacher allows his or her mood to determine the severity of a punishment, students see the teacher as unfair and become less likely to follow any of the rules. They also view the teacher as wishy-washy—someone who can be controlled by students. In classrooms of teachers who exhibit poor management skills, very little learning takes place. Though we could write an entire book on classroom management, our goal here is merely to help you take a look at your own management plan and improve upon it if necessary.

Today's activity is to look at your current management plan. Do you have one? Do you know what your rules are, and do the students know? Have you begun to set your expectations, letting students know of those expectations? Have you begun setting basic procedures with your students? Over the next three days, we will help you to devise that plan, one step at a time. Therefore, it is important to know what is already in place. And it is vital that you realize the importance of a structured management plan.

Done!

Once management is in check, all else seems to fall into place. Student behavior improves, student participation improves, student achievement improves, and the classroom hums like a well-rehearsed choir! Is your choir humming?

Think About It

Rules, rules, we make them and they break them
What can we possibly do so that, seriously, they'll take them?
Maybe if we are clear on what they can and cannot do
And set some logical consequences and actually follow through
Then seriously they'll take the rules and follow them they might
And then, by being consistent, good behavior we'll incite.

Do It

The general "rule" is that a teacher should have no more than five rules. Yet many teachers post ten or more "rules" on their classroom walls. We've learned that the most popular rule, with teachers, not with students, reads as follows: Raise your hand before speaking. Why is that the most frequently posted rule? It is because far too many teachers have never been taught the difference between a rule and a procedure. You see, talking out of turn falls under the category of procedures, not rules. (We will discuss procedures tomorrow.)

Let's define a rule as it relates to the classroom. A rule regulates a serious misbehavior. If the rule is broken, there's a consequence EVERY time. An example of a serious offense is *hitting*. Most teachers would agree that they do not want or allow students to hit one another. The rule is posted, the students know the behavior is not permitted, and there is a consequence every time the rule is broken.

For today's activity, take a look at your existing rules. Determine which of those regulate serious offenses that can never be allowed in class. Though most will agree that any amount over five is too much, most teachers have difficulty coming up with even five serious offenses. You will probably see that some behaviors you posted as rules actually fall into the category of procedures. After your rules have been determined, attach logical consequences. Share these with the students so that everyone is now clear about the rules and their corresponding consequences. Remember that the biggest challenge of having rules is enforcing them. Having too many rules will become unmanageable for you.

Done!

Students WANT to know the limits, how far they can and cannot go. Once the rules and consequences are set, posted, and understood, all you have to do is be consistent in enforcing them. When a student breaks a rule, dole out the consequence in a calm, professional manner.

Think About It

If you don't show a student how you want something done
He'll figure out his own way, and your way won't be the one!

Do It

As has often been stated, the number one problem in the classroom is not discipline. Rather, it is the lack of structured procedures. Far too many teachers overlook the importance of implementing structured procedures from day one of the school year. There are two types of procedures in the classroom—those the teacher sets and those the students set in the absence of guidance from the teacher. The latter are known as *illegal procedures*!

Procedures involve daily activities such as how to walk into the room, how to pass in papers, how to ask permission to speak, how to get into and out of groups, how to walk to lunch, what to do during a fire drill, among others. The list is long, since many daily classroom activities require procedures. Effective teachers do not establish all procedures at once. Rather, they determine the most important procedures and teach those first. Then, they slowly add to that list as students become adept at following the procedures that have already been introduced.

Your assignment today is to determine which procedures you have already established and which you need to establish. Then, remember to follow these steps when implementing procedures: Introduce the new procedure, model it by showing them exactly how you want it done, practice the procedure, continue to practice and remind them when they "forget," and remain consistent in the implementation of your procedures.

The difference between rules and procedures is that rules regulate serious offenses and procedures are simply consistent ways of doing the kinds of activities we mentioned earlier. When a student breaks a rule, you punish. When a student breaks a procedure, you practice. Being consistent, of course, is vital. If your procedure is that you will raise your hand when you need the students' attention, then that is what you must do every time. Don't resort to asking them to get quiet, threatening them, begging them to listen, reminding them that they are not paying attention, flicking the lights on and off, and so on.

Done!

Remember that a rule has a consequence, and a procedure does not. And if you're consistent, good discipline you've got!

Think About It

The speed limit sign in your neighborhood is not only for tourists! It's for you and the rest of the adults who still need reminders. YOU, the teacher, are the speed limit sign in your classroom.

Do It

Even if all the people in your neighborhood have lived there for many years and there are never any tourists passing through, the speed limit signs remain. Why? Don't you and your neighbors know the speed limit? Of course. So why won't the city remove the signs? Because even adults need constant reminders of rules and procedures. Yet, sometimes, those very same adults forget that fact and get upset when students forget rules and procedures. Those same adults say, "They know what they're supposed to do and how they're supposed to act. They're not forgetting!" Well, consider the fact that even adults who KNOW what the speed limit is don't always FOLLOW the speed limit. Both adults and children are human, and both can benefit from occasional reminders of what is expected of them.

We are not suggesting that you always look the other way and allow students not to follow your rules and procedures. In fact, since rules are meant to regulate behavior, you cannot ignore instances where students break them. The good news is that students tend to forget to follow procedures more often than they forget to follow your handful of rules. What we are suggesting is that you remain consistent with what you expect, but that you don't make the mistake of getting bent out of shape (figuratively or literally) when students falter. If they break a rule, punish them and then let it be over. If they don't follow procedures, simply provide more practice.

Your simple activity is to review your classroom management plan and be clear on the difference between your rules and your procedures. Also, be clear on letting your students know exactly what they can and cannot do and how they should and should not behave in your classroom.

Done!

Students who forget procedures and rules
Should never be made to look like fools
Just remind them when they forget from time to time
Forgetting, thank goodness, is NOT a crime!

Think About It

If the intention is good, but the follow-through is weak,
The prospect of achieving your goal is bleak.

Do It

For the past four days, we have discussed various aspects of classroom management, and you have had the opportunity to assess your own classroom management plan. Let's review a few key points:

♦ Classroom management involves all that you do to make the class run smoothly and efficiently.
♦ At its basic level, a classroom management plan consists of clear rules and procedures.
♦ Rules regulate serious offenses, and there is always a consequence when a rule is broken. Remember that you don't want to have more than a handful of rules.
♦ Procedures are consistent ways of doing certain activities such as walking into the room, asking for permission to speak, sharpening pencils, and walking to lunch.
♦ When a student does not follow a procedure, you don't punish. Rather, you provide more practice.
♦ Tell students exactly what you expect and why.
♦ Provide lots of practice and many reminders regarding the rules and procedures.

A common problem we see with teachers is this: They have good intentions in establishing management. Everyone wants good management! They establish their plans, but then they fail to follow through by remaining consistent in implementing them. So please understand that though these few days of thinking about and establishing a management plan are important, without consistent follow-through, the best-laid plans fail miserably.

Today's activity is to summarize your management plan, including listing your basic rules and procedures, explaining what it is you expect of your students in order to maximize learning, positive behavior, and student safety.

Done!

Rules are determined and defined—Check!
Procedures are determined and explained—Check!
Teacher is consistent with enforcing rules and practicing procedures—Check!

The Plan Revealed, Not Concealed

Think About It

A classroom management plan should not hold classified information
All must be revealed
Never keep it concealed
For students need to clearly know your every expectation!

Do It

In our conversations with and observations of teachers, we often find that many teachers have management plans that have been well written, well thought-out, and well placed in a desk drawer. . . . Consider a football coach going into a game with a very thorough game plan. He has thought about the plan; he has analyzed the best way to approach every possible game situation; he has written an impressive plan, and then he has placed it in his desk drawer. No one has seen the plan. On game day, he knows exactly what he expects of his players. The only problem is that his players are clueless. Nonetheless, the game begins. The players are confused, there are many penalties, and when the coach gets frustrated because players are not doing what is "expected" of them, he calls a time-out. He shares his frustrations, and he tries to motivate his players to do better. Then he sends them back into the game, but they still don't know exactly what is expected of them. Fast forward . . . they lose. Some classrooms reflect this same phenomenon. The plan has been established, but it has not been shared. Oops!

In order to guarantee the success of the classroom management plan, the teacher should ensure that the plan is understood by all involved. We recommend the following:

1. Discuss the plan with your students and give them a copy of the plan. There should be no mystery here as to what you expect and why.
2. Send a copy of the plan to parents so that they know exactly what you expect of their children in your classroom. This important step is too often overlooked by teachers.
3. Implement the plan consistently!

Done!

On rules and procedures, the teacher reflected
And she wrote and explained and shared what she expected
And to knowing what was expected, no one objected
And now discipline problems are less often detected.

Think About It

Students will hold you to your promises. Don't ever make a promise to a student unless you intend to keep it! Break a promise to a student, and you've broken your lifeline of trust with him.

Do It

Since we know that students hold us to our promises, we can use this information to benefit us and our students in the classroom. We also know that there are two things that students specifically dislike in the classroom—being yelled at by the teacher and being embarrassed by the teacher in front of their peers.

Today's activity is simple: Tell your students, "I'd like to make a couple of promises to all of you." By saying the word *promise*, you will secure their attention. Then say, "I promise that at no time during this school year will I ever raise my voice and scream at you, so relax and know that you are safe here from having anyone yell at you. I also promise that I will never intentionally embarrass you in front of your friends. Rather, I'll treat you with the respect that each of you deserves. I'm not saying I won't hold you accountable for your actions, because that's my job, and I intend to do my job. But at no time will I scream at you or intentionally embarrass you." (We always recommend using the phrase *intentionally embarrass* because it sometimes happens that a teacher embarrasses a student without intending to do so. For instance, sometimes a teacher compliments a student and the student is embarrassed.)

By making these two promises, you have accomplished the following: (1) You have helped to put your students at ease, letting them know they will not be yelled at or embarrassed in front of their peers, and (2) You have taken the options of losing your cool and embarrassing one of your students away from YOURSELF! Even though it may be tempting at times to raise your voice in anger at a student or to say or do something to embarrass a student in front of his or her peers, since you promised not to do those things, then you simply can't do them.

Done!

By promising your students not to embarrass them or yell
Your students will respect you more and behave better from bell to bell.

DAY 11

Think About It

Students like to feel that they have some ownership in the classroom and that their opinions actually matter. Teachers often tend to overlook this or simply forget to ask the students about what they think and feel. One of the best ways to find out what students think is to give them a survey on which they can anonymously state their opinions with no fear of retribution.

Do It

Today's activity involves giving the students a survey asking a few simple questions such as:

- What do you think of this class so far?
- Do you have any suggestions that you feel would help you to enjoy this class more?
- Do you feel that your opinions are valued?
- Do you feel that you are allowed to participate in this class?
- Do you feel that the teacher treats you with respect in this class?
- Does the teacher teach in a way that is interesting to you? If not, what do you think the teacher could do differently?
- Do you feel successful in this class? If not, what do you think the teacher could do to better help you succeed?
- Other suggestions:

_____

_____

_____

_____

_____

Of course, you can adapt the questions to better accommodate the grade level or subject that you teach, but the preceding should give you a good starting point. Tomorrow, we will discuss what to *do* with the results of the survey.

Done!

Sometimes giving a student a voice will help him to make a more responsible choice. And when a student feels that his opinion matters to you, he's usually more apt to actually do what you want him to do!

Think About It

Now that you've given a survey to learn what your students think and feel,
Discussing the results with them will help to seal the deal!

Do It

Okay, let's talk about what NOT to do first, when discussing the results of yesterday's survey. The odds are good that an occasional student may have provided answers such as, "I think we need to have recess all the time," or "I think we should have no homework," or "I think we should come to school one day a week." You get the idea, and you may or may not have seen something similar on a survey. Here's what we suggest. Say, "I read over the surveys, and you had some wonderful suggestions. Though I don't have time to share with you everything everyone said, I've taken the liberty of summarizing the answers so that we can discuss them."

Now discuss the results with a smile on your face. Say, for instance, "Several of you felt that you work well in groups. I have no problem putting you in groups more often as long as we continue to follow the procedures for working in groups. Thanks for the suggestion." "Some of you feel that you need more one-on-one help from me. My job is to help you succeed, so please know that you can always come to me when you need extra help." "Many of you (okay, so you may be stretching the truth a little, but we won't tell . . .) said that you like the fact that we have rules and procedures because that's the way adults handle things. You're correct! In the real world, we establish rules and procedures to keep things running smoothly. I'm glad you recognized the importance of our rules and procedures."

It is vital that you take the time to show that you value their opinions and that you will do your best to accommodate their needs, within reason, of course. When you look over these surveys, try to notice patterns. If one student feels unsuccessful, then there's no pattern there. But if more than two or three are saying that, you may want to think about what may be causing them to say that.

Done!

By letting your students express what they think, you increase the chances that you all will work in sync!

Think About It

There are times when, for a variety of reasons, you need to get a student out into the hallway, without a power struggle, in order to speak with him privately. Some students will readily follow you if you ask them to step outside with you. Others will not. Today's technique is for the student who, knowing he is in trouble, may be reluctant to step out into the hallway with you. Instead, he may choose to cause an ugly scene in class.

Do It

Let's say that a student is misbehaving in class or is doing something inappropriate. You feel it is important that you speak with her privately. However, this particular student tends to be defensive and may cause a scene if you ask her to step outside with you. What do you do? We have a trick for you. It is almost impossible to find a student who does not like to run an errand. This technique capitalizes on that fact. Here it is: Have an agreement with the teacher right across the hall from you that sounds like this: "If a student ever comes to your classroom with a sealed envelope, the envelope will be empty, but the student won't know that. I just needed to get that student out into the hallway without a power struggle. So accept the envelope and thank the student for delivering it. Thanks."

So Tina, who tends to be defensive, is misbehaving in class, and you want to speak with her privately. Simply go to your desk and get one of your already-prepared empty, sealed white envelopes and hand it to her saying, "Tina, would you take this to Mr. Thomas across the hall? Thanks." Tina takes the envelope and goes. When she returns, you are waiting for her in the hallway. She never realizes that she has been tricked because you say, "Thanks for delivering that, Tina. But before we go back inside, I'd like to speak with you about . . ." That's it. No power struggle at all. A true win–win!

Today's activity is for you to establish an agreement with a neighboring teacher to be ever-ready to receive an empty, sealed white envelope!

Done!

Teachers who are nimble and teachers who are quick
Often reach into their bags and pull out a trick
Whatever it takes to help a student to succeed
Is the motto of which they often take heed.

Think About It

Failing to plan becomes a plan to fail.
You're a ship without an anchor; you're a hammer without a nail.
So plan your lessons every day,
Stay on the path so you won't go astray,
Know why you're teaching the things that you teach,
And reap the rewards from the students you reach!

Do It

Effective teachers know that in order to have a great lesson, they need to PLAN a great lesson. The following is a list of what effective teachers take into consideration when planning a great lesson:

♦ The lesson's purpose
♦ Ideas for convincing the students that this skill is important in their lives
♦ Activities to involve students in the lesson
♦ Materials needed to teach the lesson
♦ A way to model the new skill
♦ A way to know if the lesson is successful
♦ A way to remediate for any student who does not understand the new skill

Look over this list, and compare it with your own thinking process when planning a lesson. Take care not to omit any of the entries, but feel free to add a few of your own!

Done!

You simply cannot have a great lesson without writing a great plan, so remember:

To plan a great PLAN and make each lesson better THAN
Each lesson that came BEFORE, you have to plan and plan some MORE!

DAY 15

Think About It

When your students leave your class tomorrow
What will they know or be able to do
That they don't know now and won't until you show them how?
That's your objective—now make a plan to see it through.

Do It

In planning an effective lesson, your very first step is to determine your objective, telling what the students will know or be able to do by the end of the lesson. Sometimes teachers get caught up in planning around themes or ideas or activities before becoming clear on the one objective that the lesson needs to accomplish. So the lesson lacks clarity, for both the students and the teacher.

A first grader was asked by her mother, "What did you learn in school today?" She said, "We did flipping work." The mother asked, "What do you mean?" She said, "The teacher gave us a bunch of pages stapled together and when we would finish one, we had to flip to the next and do that one. Flipping work!" Out of the mouths of babes! We don't recommend *flipping work* as an effective method of accomplishing objectives. Here's what we do recommend: Begin each lesson by telling the students exactly what they will know or be able to do by the end of the class. And use clear, measurable terms when writing your objectives in order to help you plan an effective lesson around that objective. Here are a few examples:

- The students will be able to multiply two-digit numbers.
- The students will be able to use brainstorming to generate ideas for. . . .
- The students will be able to construct a bar graph based on given information.
- The students will be able to retell the story in their own words.
- The students will explain specific events in history.

Note that the examples are written in clear and measurable terms. Now look at some of your own objectives and simply ask yourself, "Are my objectives clear and measurable?"

Done!

If asked, "What did you learn in school today?" will your students know and be able to show? Or will they shrug and say as they smirk, "Today, we just did Flipping Work"?

Planning, Part 3

Think About It

For the past two days, we've discussed the importance of planning and have provided a list of things to consider when planning. We've also talked about the plan's main component—the objective. Now you're ready to actually WRITE an effective plan, one that should not be too time-consuming, believe it or not! Effective plans don't have to be long and fancy. Rather, they just have to be clear and well organized. We'll show you how.

Do It

Here is the simplest way to write an effective plan:

1. Determine your objective and a way to convince the students that this new skill relates to their lives.
2. Determine and gather any materials you will need to teach the lesson.
3. Write your plan with most sentences beginning with "The students will . . ." This ensures a student-centered lesson.
4. Plan an introduction, a way to teach and model, a way to guide the students through practicing the new skill, a way to have them attempt the new skill on their own, a way to measure student understanding of the new skill, and a review. That's it!

Note: It is always good to have both remediation and enrichment activities planned for each lesson. In other words, what will you do with students who don't quite grasp the concept, and what will you do with students who grasp it quicker than others?

Done!

If you've followed these simple steps, you are helping to ensure a lesson that focuses on a clear objective, that involves students in every step, that relates to the lives of the students, that guides them step-by-step in the learning process, and that is measurable in its effectiveness. THAT, quite simply, is how to teach anything to anyone!

Nothing fancy or chancy, but from any perspective, it's just effective!

DAY 17

Think About It

You've determined your objective, you've written a great plan
But the fun doesn't begin until you can
See the sparkle in their eyes and the smiles on their faces
When you teach what you've planned and take them to new places!

Do It

And so the fun begins! You get to teach what you've planned. Once again, the simplest way is often the most effective way. So here is the simplest way to teach your lesson:

1. Tell the students what they will learn today and show them how the new skill relates to their lives. When we say *tell*, please understand that you can ask specific questions that lead them to be able to tell YOU why they might need this new skill.
2. Teach and MODEL the new skill. Modeling is one of the most important steps in teaching, yet it is often skipped! Often, we explain something and then have students attempt to do it without ever having SEEN it done. And the lesson falls apart then and there.
3. Practice the new skill WITH your students. At this stage, you will begin to get a good feel for student understanding or lack thereof. If you notice that many are not yet grasping the concept, continue to practice with them. You may even want to model the skill again.
4. Now have them try the new skill on their own while you monitor and provide any necessary guidance. This is also where you provide remediation for students who need it.
5. Have the students review by telling and showing YOU what they have learned. Be careful not to tell THEM.

Done!

Now that you have taught your lesson following these steps, ask yourself, "What steps could I have omitted?" Can you ever justify NOT introducing a new skill? Not teaching and modeling? Not practicing with them? Not allowing them to attempt the new skill on their own? Not reviewing in order to cement a new skill or concept? Of course you can't. Each step is vital to the lesson's success. Teach every lesson this way, and students will enjoy success each day!

Think About It

Assessment is often a dreaded word. But it need not be. In fact, it is difficult to separate the word *teaching* from the word *assessing* because you cannot effectively do one without the other. There are two basic types of assessment, formal assessment and informal assessment. Quite simply, formal assessment is graded and informal assessment is not.

Do It

In the steps you followed yesterday, you were constantly assessing—assessing student buy-in as you introduced the new skill and then assessing their understanding through all the remaining steps. By the end of the lesson, there should have been no question as to which students understood the new skill and which did not. And as you determined which did not, you were able to provide immediate remediation to those students and then determine if they needed even further remediation. This type of teaching/assessing helps to ensure that no student ever falls too far behind.

It often baffles us when we hear teachers say things like, "I gave a test and half of them failed!" That tells us that the teacher was not teaching effectively, because had he done so, he would have known almost exactly how his students would perform, due to the fact that he had been assessing their understanding since he first introduced the concept! Had he done that, he would have realized that they were not ready to be tested because he needed to do some much-needed reteaching. But the fact that we hear teachers who are often so shocked at their students' test results tells us that some teachers are just not following the simple steps we provided yesterday. So today's activity involves asking yourself one question: "Am I often shocked at my students' test results?" If your answer is yes, then that just tells you to look back at the steps we shared with you yesterday for teaching effectively and make sure that you continue to follow those steps in every lesson you teach.

Done!

You simply cannot separate teaching from assessing,
Because you assess each student as you teach.
And if you do that, there'll be no room for guessing
Because you'll know the understanding of each!

DAY 19

20-Day Reality Check

Following is a simple survey for you to complete based on all topics we have discussed until now. Your assignment today is simply to complete the survey. For each statement, write "Yes" or "No" in the right-hand column.

Survey

1	I make a special effort to wear a positive expression every day.	
2	I have devised a subtle way to change the seating arrangement in my classroom when the need arises without making these changes appear punitive.	
3	I have given some type of interest inventory in order to get to know each of my students better.	
4	I made a special effort to invite parents to back-to-school night.	
5	I have devised a classroom management plan with clearly defined rules and procedures.	
6	I am consistent in implementing my classroom management plan.	
7	I have shared my management plan with both students and parents.	
8	I have promised my students that I will never yell at them or intentionally embarrass them in front of their peers. Thus far, I have kept those promises.	
9	I have given a survey to my students soliciting their ideas, opinions, and suggestions about my class.	
10	I have established an agreement with a neighboring teacher to use the "envelope trick" from Day 14.	
11	I have had the opportunity to use the envelope trick.	
12	I write clear, measurable objectives for each lesson.	
13	I always plan for a way to make a connection between the lesson's objectives and my students' lives.	
14	I plan my lessons including the five steps provided on Day 18.	

What I Learned/What I'll Do Differently

Based on yesterday's survey results, take a few minutes to list what you have learned, what you may have already known but needed to be reminded of, what you've noticed about your students, what you will attempt to do differently in your teaching from this point forward.

DAY 21

Think About It

When you make a choice to express your distress
The students have checkmate in "classroom chess"
They have you, they know it, because you chose to show it
And when they have control, they do not acquiesce!

Do It

It is a fact that students know when they get to you ONLY if you let them know. And if you let them know that they have gotten to you, they will take advantage of their newfound power over you. **We believe that the biggest mistake that you, as a teacher, can make is to let students know that they have gotten to you personally.** You simply cannot let them know that they are leaning on your very last nerve, that you are aggravated, or that you would love to explode with anger or frustration. These are not options for professionals, ever!

We are not suggesting that you always look the other way instead of dealing with problems or that you let students "get away" with misbehavior that should be addressed. We are simply saying that you must deal with nerve-racking situations in a calm, professional manner. Never let them see you sweat! For today's activity, think about how you typically handle situations where you become frustrated or upset or personally offended by student behavior. Do your students know when they upset you? Do they know how to push your buttons? Assess your distress and rethink how you will handle these situations from today forward.

Done!

When you get angry, and you will, be careful, and then more careful still
Please don't let your anger show, 'cause if you do, then we will know
And once we know, that's it, you're through. You belong to us, not us to you
And once you're ours, we're in control. We'll never do what we are told
We'll push your buttons, we'll test your will; we'll never ever get our fill
So when you get angry, don't let it show, 'cause if you do, then we will know
And once we know, that's it, you're through. You belong to us, not us to you!

Think About It

It's a fact that in a classroom there's a direct correlation
Between a student's achievements and his teacher's expectations.

Do It

In general, people live up or down to our expectations of them. This is true in the classroom also. Students tend to live up or down to our expectations of them. If you believe a student can, he usually will. If you believe a student can't, he usually won't. This is why we want to have high, yet reasonable, expectations of each student. Countless studies have been conducted showing that teachers who have high expectations of students see higher achievement and better behavior from those students. Sadly, the opposite is also true. If you expect a student to misbehave, he usually will. If you expect him to perform poorly, he usually will. We tend to get what we expect, which might help to explain why some teachers always seem to get "the good kids" every year!

Having high expectations, however, is not enough. We have to verbalize those expectations, telling students exactly what we expect of them and convincing them that we believe they can accomplish what it is we expect them to accomplish; that they can behave the way we expect them to behave; that they can become the people we expect them to become. And then we have to guide them, step by step, in rising to those expectations. When they falter, and they will, repeat your belief in them and remind them of your expectations.

Today's activity is simple. Take note of your expectations of each of your students. Do you have high expectations for some and not for others? Are your expectations reasonable? And do you verbalize your expectations so that students know exactly what it is you expect of them? If you answered "no" to any of these, then it is probably time to rethink your expectations.

Done!

If you believe I can, I usually do. If you believe I can't, I usually don't.
So set your expectations high, and, disappoint you, I usually won't!

DAY 24

Think About It

It is not a mistake that when you walk into a restaurant or step onto an airplane or enter a store like Walmart, you are greeted with a smile. Such places of business want their customers to feel welcomed. Why is that? Because people who feel welcomed are more likely to buy what you are selling, to return to your place of business, to associate positively with your establishment.

Do It

We cannot stress enough the importance of making your students feel welcomed in your classroom every day of the school year. And the best way to do that is to greet every student every day with a smile and an enthusiastic "Hello" or "Good morning" or "How are you today?" or "I'm glad you're here." You see, students who feel that you are happy to see them are much more likely to *buy* what you are *selling*.

Now let's be honest. On any given day, it is remotely possible that you may be slightly happier to see some students than you are to see other students. That's just human nature, and it's fine as long as the students NEVER know that you aren't absolutely elated to see every one of them. And therein lies the key to the success of greeting students—you have to appear elated to see each of them, every day. If you do that on a daily basis, as opposed to just rushing them into the room saying, "Come on, get inside, let's go, get busy as soon as you walk in," then you will reap the rewards that greeting your students can provide—better behavior, happier students, more motivated students, improved achievement, and a happier teacher! Yes, a simple hello can accomplish all of that if it is offered with a smile and with enthusiasm on a consistent basis.

Today's activity involves doing what we just discussed—appearing elated to see all students as they enter the classroom, whether you are elated or you aren't. Start today and make it part of your daily routine.

Done!

A welcoming smile and a simple hello
Are always in style and they help students know
That you're happy to see them each and every day
So say hello and smile away!

My Pride and Joy

Think About It

Nothing says "I'm proud of you" better than displaying a child's work. Parents tend to put their children's drawings or report cards or good work on the refrigerator for all to see. And believe it or not, people of ALL ages like it when someone is proud of them. As teachers, we want to encourage students to take pride in their work in order to foster even better effort and accomplishment. Following is a simple way to show your pride in your students' work and accomplishments.

Do It

Gone, thankfully, are the days of teachers spending so much of their money and time on decorating the classroom walls before the students arrive on the first day. We now know that the classroom walls should consist mainly of student work, student photos, and any and everything student-related. So don't spend money on fancy decorations or countless hours decorating bulletin boards. Students care much more about seeing their own work than they do about fancy decorations.

Have several bulletin boards titled "Our Work" or "About Us" or "Things We've Learned" or "Pictures of Us," or other such titles. Be careful, of course, about displaying graded assignments, because when you do this, some students are left out. And remember that students of all ages like to see their work displayed, so this is not just for elementary classrooms. If you have some type of "Word Wall" where you display the week's vocabulary words, let the students add the new words to the wall. If you have students (and you will) who are artistic, then by all means display their artwork. With digital cameras, computers, and other electronic devices available, you can give students responsibility for selecting, gathering, and displaying evidence of projects and activities in your classroom.

By filling the classroom walls with student work, you are expressing your own pride in students; you are helping them to have pride in themselves, and you are helping them to feel like it is THEIR classroom because it is!

Today's activity is simply to look around your classroom and determine whether the walls are filled with enough student work. If not, it's an easy fix!

Done!

Displaying my work says you're proud of me
And when you're proud of me, I beam with glee
And your pride in me just might help me to be
More apt to be proud of myself, you see!

DAY 26

Think About It

Praise is one of the most valuable gifts we can give and receive. Every time we praise someone, at least two people feel better—the one who received the praise and the one who gave it! One of the simplest ways to praise students is by saying "thank you." It's a simple phrase that goes a long way in showing that you noticed a good behavior, saying that you appreciate that good behavior, and expressing that you value the actions of the student, thus valuing the student as a good person. Students who feel valued by their teachers tend to behave better.

Do It

The phrase "thank you" is uttered often in the classrooms of effective teachers. Here are a few ways to say "thank you" in the classroom:

◆ Thanks, everyone, for entering the classroom so quietly.
◆ Susan, thanks so much for remembering to do your homework.
◆ Eddie, thank you for getting busy on your assignment so quickly.
◆ Thank you, Linda, for staying in your seat today.
◆ Thanks for closing the door, Eric.
◆ Lisa, thank you for helping Liz with those problems. I know she appreciated it, but I wanted you to know that I appreciate it too!
◆ Thanks, in advance, for picking up around your desks before the bell rings. You're all so thoughtful about cleaning around your desks before you leave each day.

For today, and hopefully from this day forward, thank your students as often as possible. Notice how they respond. Notice how good they feel. Notice how effective it is![1] If you are ever concerned about embarrassing a particular student, you may want to write a note and leave it on his or her desk.

Done!

If you often say "Thank you"
I'm more likely to rank you
As a person high on my list
A list that does consist
Of people I admire and of people I respect
So thank me, thank me often
And thank YOU for your positive effect!

---

[1]Breaux and Whitaker, *50 Ways to Improve Student Behavior*, 2010. Larchmont, NY: Eye On Education.

Think About It

A teacher shared the following with us:

> Every year, I tell my students that I have a strange case of amnesia. I tell them that though I remember everything good that they do, I seem to quickly forget anything bad they do. I say, "If you do something wrong that needs to be addressed, I'll address it with you. But I want you to know that, because of my amnesia, I will forget about it the next day. So don't remind me of it or think that I will hold it against you, because I won't even remember it."
>
> My students know, of course, that I don't really have amnesia. It's just my way of letting them know that I will attack problems instead of people and I will never hold grudges against them. They're children, after all. I don't take their behavior personally. And I want them all to know that.

Do It

Consider doing what this teacher does—having a strange case of amnesia. Let your students know that you will deal with their actions, but you won't hold their actions against them. Everyone will start with a clean slate every day. There's no downside to letting your students know that you are capable of letting things go!

Done!

She remembered the good but forgot the bad
A strange case of amnesia, our teacher had
She dealt with our misgivings, then from her memory they flew
Everyone, every day, was able to start anew.

DAY 27

DAY 28

Think About It

Sometimes I just need a listening ear
I need to know that when I speak, you hear
I don't always need you to give me advice
Just listening to me can really be nice!

Do It

As teachers, we are trained to recognize and solve problems. Those are good skills to possess. Occasionally, however, we get so caught up in solving problems that we forget to *listen*. And sometimes the best solution is simply to be there to listen.

Students don't always come to us with problems or when they just need a listening ear. Often, that's because they don't know they can! It is important that we let our students know that we are here for them; that if they need to talk, we will listen. But what about the students who want you to listen to them constantly? They want your undivided attention at all times. Simply tell them, "I want to hear what everyone has to say, and I want you to know that I am here for you if you ever need to talk. However, I won't always be able to get to you right away, but I'll be available for you after class or at recess or before school or whenever. We'll find a time that works." Okay, so you're teaching, and a student who craves your undivided attention raises her hand. What she has to say has nothing to do with the lesson, and you know that nothing is wrong, so the conversation can wait. Just say, "What you have to say is important to me, but we can't discuss it right now, so remind me later, maybe after class, and we'll talk about it." Nine times out of ten, that student will go off to recess without ever telling you what she had to say. She just needed attention, and you gave it to her without appearing aggravated because what she had to say did not relate to the lesson.

Do your students all know that you are available to listen to them if they need to talk? If not, it's time to tell them!

Done!

Listen to me when I'm speaking to you
And please do not say what you think I should do
Just lend me your ear and it may become clear
That the answer lies inside of me, not you!

A Mistake for Learning's Sake

Think About It

We try to teach children that mistakes are not only okay, but that they are some of the best ways to learn and grow. We've yet to find a teacher who would argue that mistakes are wonderful learning opportunities. However, we continue to meet far too many teachers who forget to convey that message to their students. In their classrooms, mistakes are quickly pointed out and corrected, with no message saying, "Great, you made a mistake. Let's see what we can learn from that!" or "That's okay. By making mistakes, you'll get better at this skill by learning what doesn't work," or "Don't be afraid to make a mistake. It shows me that you are willing to try new things, and I admire that."

Do It

Today's activity involves two steps:

1. Take a good look at yourself and the way that you treat mistakes (and encourage students to treat mistakes) in your classroom. Ask yourself, "Have I had a discussion with my students about the fact that it is okay to make mistakes in my class? Have I discussed the importance of mistakes? Do students know that they will not be ostracized for making mistakes in this class? Do I actually encourage mistakes in this class? Do I continue to remind students, when they make mistakes, to learn and grow from these mistakes?"
2. Have a discussion with your students about mistakes. Tell them that you expect them to make mistakes in your class. Emphasize the fact that mistakes present opportunities for growth, as long as we are willing to get up after we "fall off of the bicycle" and try again.

After doing this, you will have succeeded in helping to make your students more comfortable with making mistakes and using mistakes as stepping stones to growth. For the next two days, we will focus more on making students as comfortable as possible with making mistakes so that they will be willing to take risks in your class.

Done!

When students know that mistakes enhance learning
They'll be taking more risks and better grades they'll be earning!

DAY 30

Think About It

Teachers who attempt to partake
In a persona that makes them appear opaque
And who never admit when they make a mistake
Are viewed by their students as shallow and fake.

Do It

The very best teachers make lots of mistakes. Not only do they make them, but they readily admit them. They realize the following:

♦ In order to serve as good role models, they should be models of how to handle making mistakes.
♦ Students tend to deal with mistakes in the way their adult role models deal with mistakes.
♦ People who don't make many mistakes are usually not taking many risks.
♦ Improving at anything involves taking risks.
♦ Sometimes you have to find out what does NOT work in order to discover what DOES.
♦ Teachers who admit their mistakes and demonstrate how to learn from these mistakes will be more highly respected by their students than teachers who don't.

Yesterday, you helped your students become more comfortable with mistakes by discussing that mistakes are acceptable and even desirable in your class, that students will not be ostracized for making mistakes, and that mistakes are opportunities for growth. Today, build on that discussion by telling students about some of the mistakes that you have made and how you have chosen to learn from them. From here forward, continue to point out or admit mistakes that you make so that students can learn from your example.

Done!

When students see that even YOU
Make mistakes sometimes in things you do
And when they learn from you that mistakes are okay
Leading us toward a better way
They'll be more willing to take more chances
And handle their mistakes in a way that enhances
Learning and growing and aspiring and achieving
And then, in themselves, they just might start believing!

Mistakes You Make

Think About It

A sad fact is that many students are afraid of being anything less than perfect. Many, realizing they can't possibly live up to this unrealistic expectation, simply give up and pretend not to care. These students are often heard saying, "I don't care." But they DO care—so much that they're afraid to make mistakes for fear of appearing incompetent or unintelligent or unpopular or you name it. Other students put so much pressure on themselves to be perfect that they lose their childhood in the process, constantly worrying, feeling stressed, and suffering physically, socially, and emotionally. Sometimes, they feel pressured by adults to be perfect. Regardless of the reasons, it is never good when a student feels he cannot make mistakes.

Do It

For the past two days, you have helped to shed a more positive light on the act of making mistakes. You have helped to take the pressure off of your students, at least in your classroom. You have helped them to trust that mistakes are "okay" in your classroom. Yes, we try our best and making mistakes can be disappointing, but if we treat them as opportunities to learn, the disappointment quickly gives way to the pride of accomplishment.

Today's activity involves a little role play. First, have a brief discussion with your students about the kinds of mistakes they sometimes make. Make a list for all to see. Examples might include:

♦ Answering incorrectly
♦ Misspelling a word
♦ Missing a step or two in solving a problem
♦ Not studying for a test
♦ Making a bad behavioral choice

After you've generated a list, have them role play both appropriate and inappropriate ways of handling the mistakes that they have listed. Discuss the consequences of both sides of the coin—the appropriate way, and the inappropriate way. By doing this, you are helping them not only to feel more comfortable with making mistakes, but you are also providing them with options for handling these situations effectively.

Done!

Continue to remind them, throughout the year, that mistakes are part of learning as opposed to things to fear!

Saying "Pass" in This Class

Think About It

Just because you have helped to make students more comfortable with taking risks and making mistakes in your class over the past few days, it does not mean that they will suddenly become anxious to make mistakes and take risks. It simply means they'll be a little less frightened and feel a little less pressured. But still, even for adults, it is not always easy to take risks, especially in front of our peers. As teachers, we want our students to feel as comfortable and relaxed as possible in our classrooms. Students who feel comfortable in an environment behave better, work harder, and are more apt to take risks than students who feel fearful, ostracized, or threatened in their environments. Thus, we want to provide yet another way of helping you to help your students feel as comfortable as possible in your classroom.

Do It

We have seen this technique work wonders for many teachers over the years—the option for students to say, "Pass." The teacher simply says the following to the students:

> As you know, it is important to me that you know I will never intentionally embarrass you in this class. I want you to feel as safe and relaxed as possible in order for you to learn as much as possible. Therefore, I am giving you the option to say "Pass" in this class. If I ever call on you to answer a question and, for some reason, you don't want to answer, you may simply say, "Pass." Saying "Pass" may mean you don't know the answer. It may mean you need a little more time to think. It may mean you aren't feeling well. I won't ask you what it means. I simply want for you not to ever feel caught off guard.

NOTE: This technique ONLY works in classrooms where teachers make every effort to put students at ease. If a teacher leans toward being negative with students, this technique will not work. Students will take advantage and just say "Pass" in order to push the teacher's buttons. But in the hands of caring, effective teachers, students do not take advantage, but rather appreciate the opportunity to say "Pass" just in case they ever get caught off guard for whatever reason. Give your students the opportunity to say "Pass."

Done!

Everyone, from time to time, occasionally needs a "pass"
So give me the chance to have a "pass" in this class
And we'll be less likely to reach an impasse!

Think About It

Do the following two poems ring a little too true?

Dear Parent:
Your child did something awful today while he was in my room
I hate to have to write this note, so filled with doom and gloom
But I feel that I must send it because I thought you'd like to know
And I'm hoping you can talk to him and punish him harshly—So
That he begins behaving now and causes me less trouble
If we don't nip this in the bud, the trouble may soon double!

Dear Teacher:
I got your note and spoke with my son who said he did not do it
He says no matter what he does, somehow you misconstrue it
So behavior needs to change, all right, that behavior being your own
We'll expect that you apologize in order to atone!

Do It

Announce to your students that you will no longer write notes to their parents if they misbehave. This will be met with smiles and sighs of relief. Tell them, "Instead, you will write the notes. You're old enough and mature enough now, and I'm sure you would rather write that type of note yourself than to have me write it." Be careful not to say this in a sarcastic tone, but rather act as if you are doing a favor for them. You'll be amazed at the results! The next time a student does something that warrants alerting her parents, simply say, "I know your realize that your parents need to know about this, so go ahead and write a note telling them what happened." You, of course, will sign the note and request a parent signature beneath the student's signature. You'll never again have a parent contacting you to say his child did not commit the act in question, because the child admitted it in her own handwriting! This, to parents, is much less threatening and usually more believable.

Done!

If a child writes her own note to her mom or to her dad
Admitting in her own words that she did something bad
Her parents will believe it, and although they may be mad
Her behavior might improve even more than just a tad!

---

[2]Breaux and Whitaker, *50 Ways to Improve Student Behavior*, 2010. Larchmont, NY: Eye On Education.

DAY 33

Bet on the Teacher's Pet

Think About It

The *teacher's pet* is a term used to describe a student who gets special attention from the teacher. The teacher seems to favor this student over others. Students resent it when a teacher shows obvious favoritism toward one or more students to the exclusion of others. Who can blame them? Everyone wants to feel special. Even the toughest students secretly want their adult role models to care about them. Is it human nature to like some students more than others? Yes. Are some students easier to like than others? Yes. But the students CANNOT know this!

Do It

Consider the fact that we like those who like us. Knowing this, it is important for teachers to make their students feel "liked." We suggest that you go a step beyond that, however. We suggest that you do what the best teachers do and make each and every student feel like your favorite student. It's easy enough to do.

- Greet all students as they enter the class each day. Use their names. This means a LOT to students.
- Make sure that you don't show favoritism to a select few students.
- Make an effort to take an interest in every one of your students, getting to know something personal about each, allowing each to do special "favors" for you from time to time.
- Involve every student, every day, in every lesson you teach.
- Tell all students goodbye when they leave. Again, use their names.

Done!

I have a class of 30 students, and each one is my pet
By making each feel special, their best I'm sure to get!

I Like It!

Think About It

If you want to make your students feel that you actually do listen to them, then do just that—listen to them. Give them the opportunity to tell you what they like about your class so far. This will help them see that you value their opinions and that you are open to suggestions. This is not to say, of course, that you let them have or do whatever they want. But some of the best suggestions we ever get come from our students!

Do It

Today's activity is simply to ask your students to list five things they like about this class. Some answers will be duplicated. For instance, several students may list that they like group work or a certain game you play with them. List the results here. You'll discuss these results in a couple of days with them. Tell them that.

DAY 35

_____

_____

_____

_____

_____

_____

_____

_____

_____

_____

_____

_____

_____

_____

Done!

After you have collected their lists, compile them and decide how you will address these results with your students day after tomorrow.

DAY 36

Think About It

Yesterday, you had your students name activities they enjoy in your classroom. It is equally important to allow them to tell you what they don't enjoy. Knowing this may help you to see patterns of what does and does not motivate students to learn and achieve. Now let's say a student says he does not like tests. We are not suggesting that you stop testing! But by questioning students as to their likes and dislikes, you may find that some students suffer from test anxiety, and you can then help them to overcome that. As we said, knowing what they don't like is every bit as important as knowing what they do like.

Do It

Today's activity is simply to ask your students to list five things they do not like about this class. Some answers will be duplicated. List the results here. You'll discuss these results tomorrow. Tell them that.

_____

_____

_____

_____

_____

_____

_____

_____

_____

_____

_____

_____

_____

_____

_____

_____

Done!

After you have collected their lists, compile them and decide how you will address the results with your students tomorrow.

Think About It

Have you ever filled out a survey and then wondered, "Will anyone even look at this?" We all like (and deserve) to be heard—to know that someone is listening and at least considering our thoughts and feelings. Our students deserve no less!

Do It

Today, take some time to sit with your students and discuss the results of the previous two days' activities where they each listed five things they do and do not like about your class. Be sure to handle this diplomatically. For instance, let's say that one or more students stated, "I don't like that we can't talk to our friends whenever we want." When you discuss it, say something like, "I understand, completely, why you would want to talk to your friends whenever you want. That's human nature. But I also know you understand why this isn't possible. . . ." And go on to explain the need for focused learning time. Don't appear upset by anything that someone has written, even if you are.

A key to the success of this activity is to make a few changes based on student suggestions. If someone says, "I think we should play more games," then say something like, "You're right on target. You've noticed that we all learn better when we are actively involved, and learning games tend to involve everyone more. So I'm taking your wonderful suggestion and will be adding more learning games to my instruction. Thanks for bringing that to my attention."

Done!

You have succeeded in allowing your students to be heard! After implementing this activity, many teachers decide to do this more often, allowing their students more input in how the class is run.

If they OWN it, they're less likely to BEMOAN it!

Think About It

We'd like to invite you to come in and see
Things we have accomplished—Proud of us, you'll be
What you see will excite you, and that, we guarantee
So please, please dear principal, come and see!

Do It

One of the best ways to get students on your side (and you NEED them to be on your side) is to convince them that you are proud of them. And one of the best ways to express your pride in them is to invite the principal to come in and see something wonderful that they are doing or have done.

Today's activity is simple: Send a written invitation to your principal, inviting him or her to come in and see something special that your students are accomplishing. Make a big deal about this with your students. And we are talking about ALL grade levels! Have them help you with the invitation, tell them you can't wait to show them off to the principal, and then have a student, or even a group of students, deliver this invitation to the office. We suggest that you tell your principal about this in advance so that he or she will be available to accept the invitation when it is delivered and will play along, making this seem like a big deal. We repeat that this is for ALL grade levels. We never get too old to appreciate being appreciated! Set a time with your principal, so that you know when he or she will be arriving. This will give you time to prepare with your students. Yes, you want them to be prepared to show off, to display their best work, to be on their best behavior. This will help to guarantee the success of the activity, which is exactly what you want—to do what all great teachers do—to continually find new ways of setting your students up for success!

You will be amazed at the results. And you will be accomplishing the following: (1) You will be expressing your pride in your students. That always helps to get them on your side. (2) You will allow your principal to see that good things are happening in your class. (3) Your pride and your administrator's pride in your students will help them to take pride in themselves. Win, win, win!

Done!

Tell them and show them that you're proud of what they do, and they'll be more likely to do what you want them to do! So express your pride and watch their smiles get wide!

What's the Picture?

Think About It

Have you ever put together a jigsaw puzzle? The task can be quite daunting. But at least you know how the finished product will look because a picture of it is on the box. In fact, the picture is what attracted you to the puzzle. Now consider the fact that trying to teach a student something without luring him in with a "picture" of the finished product is like trying to put together a jigsaw puzzle without first seeing the picture! Too often, teachers attempt to teach without first "showing the picture," and they end up battling with frustrated, unsuccessful, unmotivated students.

Do It

Let's say you're teaching, in math, how to calculate *perimeter*, *area*, and *volume*. Please don't teach the formulas until students know how these skills relate to real life. Oftentimes, we see a teacher drawing a rectangle on the board and telling students that the way to figure out the area is to multiply the length times the width. The students practice the skill, but they don't see the picture or purpose, so the activity seems meaningless.

Instead, do something like this: Lay out a piece of cardboard. Paint it green if you like, as this will be a back yard. Say, "This is your new back yard, and we're going to be putting a swimming pool into it." Help the students figure out the size and location of the pool. You can use a baking pan as the swimming pool. Cut the cardboard to accommodate the pool. Then, calculate the volume of water for the pool. You can also put a fence around the pool. Do you see how they will be calculating *perimeter*, *area*, and *volume*? Students LOVE this type of activity! You can then give them their own cutouts of varying cardboard templates and various pools (pans). Each can create his or her own back yard and install a pool, fence, and such, accompanied by notes explaining *area*, *perimeter*, and *volume*. They can bring in actual grass and make model trees, pool furniture, and so on. You'll be amazed at your young landscape architects!

Done!

If I know what the task will "look like" when I've finally finished
My motivation will be increased, and my frustrations will be diminished.

20-Day Reality Check

Following is a simple survey for you to complete based on all topics we have discussed since the previous 20-Day Reality Check. Your assignment today is simply to complete the survey. For each statement, write "Yes" or "No" in the right-hand column.

Survey

1	I am careful never to let students know when they have pushed my buttons or upset me personally.	
2	I have high, yet reasonable, expectations of my students.	
3	I enthusiastically greet students, every day, as they enter my classroom.	
4	Student work is prominently displayed throughout my classroom.	
5	I use the phrase "thank you" often in my classroom.	
6	I have "amnesia," which allows my students to start fresh each day.	
7	I try to be a good listener with all my students.	
8	I make every effort to help my students feel comfortable with making mistakes. I also share some of my own mistakes with my students.	
9	I have implemented the "Pass" technique from Day 32.	
10	I have students write their own notes to their parents when they have done something that warrants informing their parents.	
11	I make an effort to make each student feel as though he or she is my favorite.	
12	I allow my students to share what they like/do not like about my class.	
13	I provide students with a "picture" of what they will be learning each day (as discussed on Day 39).	
14	I occasionally invite an administrator in and allow students to share their accomplishments.	

What I Learned/What I'll Do Differently

Based on yesterday's survey results, take a few minutes to list what you have learned, what you may have already known but needed to be reminded of, what you've noticed about your students, what you will attempt to do differently in your teaching from this point forward.

_____

_____

_____

_____

_____

_____

_____

_____

_____

_____

_____

_____

_____

_____

_____

_____

_____

_____

_____

_____

_____

_____

_____

_____

_____

_____

_____

_____

Think About It

Some parents are actively involved in the education of their children. Others are not. Some parents readily answer any phone calls you make or respond to any notes you send home. Others do not. But ALL parents like to hear good news from their children's teachers. So today, we encourage you to do just that.

Do It

Write a simple note to the parents of all your students. Just write one note, not one to every parent. The note might say something like this:

Dear Parents:

I'm excited to let you know about some of the wonderful things that we are accomplishing in class this year. Here are a few of which we are especially proud:

1. _____
2. _____
3. _____
4. _____
5. _____

It is a pleasure to be able to work with your children. Thank you for your ongoing support. Please feel free to contact me at

_____ .

Sincerely,

_____

Done!

Make a copy of this note for all your students and ask them to deliver these to their parents. That's it. By doing this, you are sending good news home, you are endearing yourself to the parents of your students, you are displaying your love of children and teaching, and you are endearing yourself to your students. Parents never scoff at good news about their children. And when parents believe you care about their children, they are much more likely to work cooperatively with you. There's simply no downside to sending these types of notes home!

DAY 42

Think About It

Have you ever experienced road hypnosis while driving? If you have, you know that the best thing you can do is to stop the car, get out, and walk around a little. Have you ever found yourself drifting off while listening to a speech? Have you ever fallen asleep while involved in a conversation with someone? Hopefully not, but you get the point. When something becomes monotonous, we can lose our focus quite easily. And when we don't move around much, it is easy to fall asleep. That is why all of us have experienced falling asleep while watching television, even if what we were watching was interesting.

The same concept applies to the classroom. When students have been involved in a monotonous task, they tend to lose their focus. If they haven't moved around much for an extended period of time, they may even be tempted to enter a dream state!

Do It

One of the secrets of effective teachers is that they know the importance of providing frequent breaks for students in order to keep them involved, focused, and awake. Sometimes, the break involves a teacher saying something like, "Okay, you have 25 seconds to stand up and stretch." Of course, these teachers also have a very clear procedure established for getting the students back into their seats and quiet when the break is over. Sometimes, the break involves a teacher saying, "Turn to the person next to you and take a minute to discuss your feelings on the information we have just learned." Yet another example is a teacher saying, "Everyone get up, walk to the front of the class, and sit in a semicircle around me for this next activity."

We could think of many more examples, but the bottom line is that it is important to keep activities moving, to provide occasional stretch breaks, to keep students physically moving. Avoid monotony in order to avoid classroom hypnosis.

Done!

Keep me awake by giving me a break
And keep me moving so that my focus will be improving
And keep me participating and relating and creating
And soon you'll be amazed at how seldom I'll now appear dazed!

DAY 43

I'm Here, Dear

Think About It

Do you have someone in your life—a spouse, a friend, a family member, a colleague—to whom you can go if you have a problem, if you need to blow off steam, if you want to share something exciting that has happened to you, or if you just need someone to listen? Chances are that you do. And just knowing that that person is there for you is sometimes enough because it's comforting to know someone cares. Believe it or not, some students do not have any such person in their lives. And even those who do can always benefit from yet another person who cares and is willing to listen or provide support. Be that other person!

Do It

Your students need to feel as though you are in their corner and that you are there for them if they need you. Even if they never come to you, that's okay. It strengthens the bond between teachers and students when students trust their teachers, when they know they can go to their teachers in a time of need or when they want to share a bit of good news with someone who'll be genuinely happy for them and proud of them. When you can manage to establish that kind of bond with students, they will behave better; they will try harder, and they will do basically anything you need them to do.

Don't assume they know you are in their corner and that you will be available to speak with them when and if they need you. Tell them! Spell it out for them. Take the time today to say, "I want you all to know that I care about you, not just as my students, but as individuals. What happens in your lives matters to me. And I want you to know that if I can ever be of help, if I can ever offer you any advice if you're struggling with a problem, if I can ever lend my ear if you need to talk, don't hesitate to come to me. I'll always make time for you. I can't promise I'll always have an answer for you, but I'll certainly try to help you in any way I can."

Done!

It's good to know you're there for me if ever I should need
To talk about a problem or to tell about a deed
Just knowing I can go to you really means a lot
So thanks for being on my side—my admiration and trust, you've got!

My Hero, Part 1

Think About It

Everyone has heroes—people we admire and often try to emulate because of their extraordinary deeds or personality traits. Heroes can be anyone—from a parent to a teacher to a friend to a television personality to a heroic figure in history. Because children are in constant need of positive role models, they begin identifying their heroes early in life.

Do It

Take a few minutes to discuss, with your students, the characteristics of heroes:

♦ What makes someone a hero?
♦ Can anyone be a hero?
♦ List some qualities you would consider heroic.
♦ Whom would you most wish to be like, and why?

Have your students write about one or two of their heroes—telling who they are and why they are considered heroic to the student. Let students know that they will each be asked to share one of their heroes with the class over the next three days. We have spread this out over three days so that the activity should take only a few minutes each day. We DO realize you have lots to accomplish each day. But spending just a few minutes helping your students to become better people is worth it!

This activity encourages students to think about noble qualities in people they admire. An added benefit for you is that learning this information about each student will help you to get to know each on a more personal level. Knowing the character traits a person admires tells you a lot about that person. This activity can provide valuable insight into what makes your students tick!

Done!

Telling me of someone you admire
Helps me to better know YOU
For when someone lights your spirit afire,
You tend to emulate what they do.

My Hero, Part 2

For today, allow a third of your class to share information about one of their heroes with the class. Give each student about 30 seconds to share. You may want to take notes for yourself based on each student's hero here:

_____

_____

_____

_____

_____

_____

_____

_____

_____

_____

_____

_____

_____

_____

_____

_____

_____

_____

_____

_____

_____

_____

_____

_____

_____

_____

_____

DAY 46

My Hero, Part 3

For today, allow another third of your class to share information about one of their heroes with the class. Again, you may want to take notes for yourself based on each student's hero:

_____

_____

_____

_____

_____

_____

_____

_____

_____

_____

_____

_____

_____

_____

_____

_____

_____

_____

_____

_____

_____

_____

_____

_____

_____

_____

_____

_____

_____

DAY 47

My Hero, Part 4

For today, allow the final third of your class to share information about one of their heroes with the class. You may want to take notes for yourself based on each student's hero here:

_____

_____

_____

_____

_____

_____

_____

_____

_____

_____

_____

_____

_____

_____

_____

_____

_____

_____

_____

_____

_____

_____

_____

_____

_____

_____

_____

_____

_____

_____

DAY 48

Think About It

Teaching, it is often said, is one of the few professions that looks much the same as it did thirty, forty, and even more years ago. Medicine doesn't, thank goodness. But that's not to suggest that everything doctors did or suggested thirty, forty, fifty years ago was bad or wrong. At the time, they did their best with what they knew. Even today, some of the suggestions they made and techniques they used years ago are still considered effective. "An apple a day . . ." still holds true, since eating fruit is still considered to promote good health. Teaching is much the same. We are not suggesting that all teaching methods of days past are passé and won't work in today's classroom. For example, being consistent and establishing clear rules and procedures worked back then, and it still works today. But many of the techniques of years ago, we now know, are not effective in today's world.

So why is it that, even though we know new and better ways to teach students today, many teachers still hold on for dear life to the old ways of doing things? Why is it that their teaching looks like it did when they first started teaching? The answer is, quite simply, comfort zones. We all have them. They are the reasons we keep doing things in our lives that don't work or remain in miserable job settings or stay in bad relationships, for example. Comfort zones. But just as we expect doctors and surgeons to break out of their comfort zones and continue to learn and grow and change, we should expect no less of ourselves as teachers.

Do It

Today's activity simply involves listing two or three areas of your teaching that are a little old and tired and could possibly use some spicing up. Just list them. We'll help you to move out of your comfort zones over the next few days.

Done!

A sense of familiarity is like a dear, dear friend to me
For it comforts me when I feel safe and content
But if all things new and different, I never allow life to send to me
I'll freeze like an ungreased tin man, stiff and bent.

DAY 50

Think About It

Lecturing, meaning in the boring sense where teachers talk and students simply take notes, is considered one of the least effective methods of instruction. However, it's still one of the most often used teaching techniques. Having students simply read a chapter with no purpose other than answering the questions at the end of the chapter is simply not effective. Round robin reading, where each student reads a paragraph, pretty much guarantees that one student is paying attention: the student reading.

So what about having meaningful, interactive discussions? What about tearing a chapter apart and analyzing it in small segments, discussing and interpreting and analyzing? What about USING a story to apply skills as opposed to simply reading the story aimlessly? What about allowing students to use the technology now so readily available to them to supplement any and all types of instruction? We're not suggesting throwing away textbooks. We're suggesting rethinking how you are actually using them.

Do It

Yesterday, we had you list two or three areas of your teaching that could use some spicing up. Today, we ask that you come up with one way for each of those you listed—just one way—to improve in each area. Actually think about why it is that each of those areas is not as effective as you'd like. Then make a small change toward improvement. Nothing has to be drastic. You may be accustomed to having students read an entire chapter and then answering questions. Instead, you might decide to try breaking the chapter into segments and coming up with a given purpose for each segment, allowing students to work cooperatively to interact with the assigned text, followed by a group discussion. That one simple change can make a big difference in student interaction, understanding, and achievement.

Done!

Change it, rearrange it
Step outside your comfort zone
Juice it up and spruce it up
Take a step into the great unknown!

Out with the Old, Part 3

Think About It

"Can" the Lists
On Monday you gave me 20 words for Friday's vocabulary test
I wrote them five times every night and I studied my very best
On Friday, I was well prepared to spit them back to you
I got them all, word for word, as I was expected to do
But I have a confession to make to you—despite the grade I earned
Those words have left my memory now; no vocabulary have I learned
You see, I never used the words or spoke them in conversation
So I guess we both just wasted our time—what an awful revelation!
So next time, leave the lists alone; make me use the words
If you don't, then I'll soon lose them; they'll fly away like birds
I want to keep whatever I learn; I want to deserve the grade I earn
I want to be smart and witty and wise, but wisdom doesn't come when I memorize
I really do want to learn, you know, so "can" the lists and watch me grow![3]

Do It

The sentiment of the preceding poem is familiar to anyone who has ever been a teacher or student. For years, students have been given lists of words to memorize—a dreaded task with dire results. Our suggestion to you is that you "can" the lists and begin teaching vocabulary in more effective ways—where students actually add new words to their vocabularies, beyond the week of the test. In any subject area, vocabulary lessons should consist of a variety of ways that students decipher word meanings, practice using the words, discuss the words and concepts relating to those words, solve problems using the words, are provided opportunities to incorporate the vocabulary into their writing and speaking, and so on. Memorizing lists of words has never been effective and never will be.

Done!

Students really do want to learn, you know, so "can" those lists and watch them grow!

---

[3]Breaux, *101 Poems for Teachers*, 2010. Larchmont, NY: Eye On Education.

Think About It

If you asked people to tell you whose faces appear on a five, ten, twenty, and hundred dollar bill, most would be unable to do that. Yet most people handle bills on a daily basis. In fact, most of us had to memorize the faces on the bills in school. But almost all of us have forgotten. Why? Because you don't need to know whose face is on a bill in order to spend it! You simply need to look at the number on the bill to know its value. Ask most people to name all the presidents of the United States and they will fail miserably. Why? Because, even though they memorized that list somewhere back in their school days, they have forgotten the information. The good news is that, in today's world, information is readily available through technology. What's important is to know HOW to find information when you need it. The bad news is that far too many teachers still require students to memorize useless facts in order to spit them back on Friday's test.

We are not suggesting that it would be wrong to mention, in a lesson, whose faces appear on certain bills of currency, discussing who these people were in history and why they were chosen to be represented on the currency. We ARE suggesting that you not require students to memorize that kind of information.

Do It

Today's activity is simple: Think of something that you typically require students to memorize. Then, ask yourself the following question: Do students need to memorize this information in order to be able to use a particular skill in life? If your answer is yes, then it's meaningful memorization. For instance, if you are requiring students to memorize, in reading lessons, those words known as sight words—words that don't follow typical phonetic patterns or words that occur most frequently in reading and should be learned by sight— then that's meaningful memorization. But if you're requiring students to memorize facts that they'll forget as soon as they take the test, you may want to rethink your approach.

Done!

Determine the causation for using memorization
And if it lacks connotation, consider cessation!

Think About It

When there is a behavior problem in the classroom, we are usually dealing with one of two things: It is either a student problem or a teaching problem. When it's a student problem, this means the teacher and the teaching or management techniques have nothing to do with the problem. When it's a teaching problem, this simply means that there is something the teacher is or is not doing that has quite possibly fueled the misbehavior. Determining the cause will help to determine the solution.

Do It

Remember that you cannot ever assume that a problem is a "student problem" unless you are certain of the following: (1) procedures are evident; (2) organization is evident; (3) positive rapport with the students is evident; (4) teacher enthusiasm is evident; (5) there is no down time when students have nothing to do; (6) the teacher ensures success for all students; (7) lessons are well prepared, relate to the lives of the students, and actively involve students; (8) every student is treated with dignity; and (9) the teacher does not allow students to push his or her buttons.

If ALL (not some) of these are in place, then you are dealing with a student problem. But if even one of those listed is not in place, you must first get it in place to determine if the problem is student related. Therefore, your assignment is to take this list and ensure that all of these conditions are in place. Then, if you determine that a problem is teaching related, simply make an adjustment to your teaching. If you determine that a problem is student related, deal with the student.

We continue to find that when all of these conditions are in place in a teacher's classroom, behavior problems are minimal.

Done!

When you pause to determine the misbehavior's cause
The solution is clearer and harmony is nearer.

DAY 53

The Choice of a Calm Voice

Think About It

There is no question about it—the louder you speak, the less others listen. A soft, calm voice tends to express caring and concern. A loud voice tends to express aggravation and agitation. In the classroom, students respond much better to teachers who present themselves in a calm, controlled manner, speaking in a calm voice, even and especially when a student is out of control. Students unknowingly mimic the demeanors of their teachers. This is why the same students can act differently in different teachers' classrooms. In the classrooms of teachers who tend to speak loudly and appear less than calm, behavior problems are more evident. Effective teachers are aware of this, and they make every effort to appear and sound calm. It does not mean that they always *feel* calm and in control. Rather, they make a choice to *appear* calm and in control. And one of the very best ways to appear calm is to speak with a calm, soothing voice.

Do It

Today, we would like for you to assess your own voice by answering the following questions:

- Do I tend to speak loudly in my classroom during times of crisis when a student is misbehaving?
- Do I tend to speak loudly in my classroom while I'm teaching?
- Do I make an effort to portray a calm demeanor at all times in my classroom?
- Am I aware that the louder a student gets, the softer my voice must become in order to deal with him effectively?
- Could someone occasionally walk down the hall and hear me raising my voice with a student or my class in an attempt to gain control?
- Does my voice ever express aggravation and irritation in the classroom?

If you have determined that your voice could use some calming, then begin today to practice that. You'll notice an immediate difference in the behavior of your students.

Done!

A soothing voice is like a balm
It comforts me and keeps me calm
So speak to me in a calmer way
And better behavior is what I'll display.

Think About It

Consider the fact that when most students are sent to the office, it's for negative reasons. (We'll discuss more of the negative reasons on Day 62.) How many times, in your own schooling, were you sent to the office because your teacher wanted to make someone in the office aware of something good that you were doing or had accomplished—a good behavior, an academic accomplishment, an award you received either in or out of school, a good deed you had performed? How many of your classmates were sent to the office for any or all of those same reasons? If you were to "guesstimate" a percentage, you would probably come up with a very low number. We often ask this question of teachers and students and find that being sent to the office for positive reasons is a rare occurrence. Why do you think that is?

Do It

Start a new trend today. When a student does something good, send him to the office! Send a little note along with him that says something like, "John received an award in my class for having the most improved behavior this week. I just wanted you to know what a good job he is doing." That's it. If the principal or assistant principal is not available, that's okay. He can simply leave the note for them to find when they return. If an administrator is available, then he or she will have the opportunity to pat John on the back for a job well done. This little technique makes a big difference. Just watch how much better John's behavior becomes. And no student is too old to do this. We all like to be complimented and recognized for a job well done!

Make it a part of your routine. At least once a week, send a student to the office for a positive reason. Trust us when we tell you that any administrator will welcome this kind of good news!

Done!

You sent me to the office when I did something good
To let others know that, being good, I could
And they praised me which made me want to be even better
For fostering good behavior, you're a real trendsetter!

DAY 56

Think About It

Though students never actually believe that you are a real, human person (and that is why you become famous in the grocery store!), and though we do not suggest that you clue students in on every aspect of your life outside of school, we highly recommend a "Teacher Feature" in your room—a poster or a bulletin board displaying things pertaining to you.

By taking a small space in the room to feature yourself, you are letting students know that you are qualified to teach them, that you are, in fact, a real person, that you are proud of being a teacher, that you were once a student, too, that you have a family, and so on. By becoming just a little more human to your students, they will connect with you better.

Do It

Create your own "Teacher Feature" and display it proudly in your classroom. After you display it, don't say a thing. Just wait for your students to see it and then watch their reactions. You may be amazed at just how amazed they are by you!

Items to include in your "Teacher Feature" might include:

♦ A picture or two of yourself when you were in school
♦ One of your old report cards (if you so dare)
♦ Pictures of you with your family
♦ Copies of your high school and college diplomas
♦ A copy of an award or two you may have received
♦ A picture of you with your current students
♦ A picture of you engaged in one of your favorite hobbies
♦ A short list of goals you would like to accomplish in your life
♦ A list of reasons you love teaching

Done!

Show that you are proud of who you are and what you do
And students will respond favorably and even emulate you!

That's What I Like About You

Think About It

How do you feel when someone says something nice about you or notices something you do well and comments on it? Well, imagine if, as a student, one day you had walked into class and your teacher handed you a piece of paper with a little note mentioning one thing he or she really liked about you! Just imagine how you would feel.

We know of an amazing high school teacher who shared something wonderful she does with her students every year. We often share her idea with other teachers, at all grade levels, who continue to enjoy very positive results when they implement it in their own classrooms. Therefore, we'd like to share it with you.

Several times a year, she simply writes a short note to each of her students telling them one thing she really admires about him or her. Her students can't wait to read these, their smiles and pride are evident, and they hold onto these as if they were actual gold. Many of her former students have shared with her that they still have theirs and intend to keep them forever!

This particular teacher is a high school teacher, but we'd like to note that teachers of all levels use this technique and love it.

Do It

Today's activity is obvious—try the activity we have just shared with you. Keep the notes brief—just a couple of sentences at most. Then sit back and enjoy your students' reactions!

Done!

Just one little note
Written just for my eyes to see
And on it, you simply wrote
Of something you liked about me
But simple as it was
It touched my heart and soul
It has become a treasure to me
Worth more than a pot of gold!

Stop for a Photo Op

Think About It

Students of all ages love seeing pictures of themselves. That's a fact. Another fact is that when you display a picture of someone, it sends a message that you care about that person and that you're proud of him or her. Isn't that the message we want to send to each of our students every day? So take these facts and use them to both your advantage and theirs in the classroom. Begin taking photos of students engaged in group activities, receiving recognition or awards, posing and smiling, working at their desks, engaged in experiments or demonstrations, and so on. Then begin to display these photos throughout your classroom. Change the photos as often as you'd like, but always be careful not to leave anyone out. Make sure everyone has his or her photo displayed in your room. If they'd like to bring in their own photos to display, let them do that also. Making the classroom represent your students expresses the fact that this is their classroom, their home away from home each day. Just as parents love to display photos of their family throughout their homes, make sure you display pictures of your students (your school family) throughout your classroom. The results will be nothing but positive.

Do It

You don't have to be a photographer, nor do you have to hire one. Just start taking pictures of your students engaged in various activities, and begin posting those on the wall. Just to prove that students will love this idea, take one picture today of your class and post it on the wall. Then notice how many of them go to look at it and how often they do so. This one photo should be enough to convince you to start adding more. Feel free to delegate this task to your students. Each week, assign a different student to be the photographer.

In environments where teachers express that they care, students behave and try harder there!

Done!

You put my picture on the wall
For everyone to see
The fact that you thought to do that
Says you obviously care about me
It says you think I'm special
Special enough to display
So since you think so highly of me
I'll give you my best each day!

Small Bites Are Easier to Swallow

Think About It

Yes, the smaller the bite, the easier it is to swallow and the better it is for your digestion. Teaching in small bites has the same effect! If you were learning to snow ski for the very first time, wouldn't it be best if your instructor allowed you to become successful one small "bite" at a time? Don't you think it would feel good to GET good at standing in your skis first before actually heading down the mountain? And wouldn't you want to become adept at skiing down a very minor slope before attempting something steep? That's just common sense. Yet sometimes, in the classroom, we give too much information too fast, and then we scratch our heads when the students just don't seem to get it. The problem is that they're overwhelmed, they don't feel successful, and they give up. Then we call them unmotivated and lazy.

The fact is that if you want to teach in a way that students understand, you have to set them up for success by teaching in small bites. Think of it this way: Small steps and plenty of "reps." You won't *cover* as much material this way, but what you teach will STICK! And, most importantly, teaching in small bites helps to ensure improved student success. When they become successful with step one, they take another step, but not UNTIL they become successful with step one do they attempt step two. Until a student is successful with addition, attempting to teach him multiplication is futile. Oh, he may memorize his multiplication tables, but he'll never be able to apply the skill of multiplying because he won't know what he's doing or why he's doing it.

Effective teachers teach concepts using very simple steps. They exemplify how to simplify!

Do It

Remember: Small steps and plenty of "reps." Look at one, just one, of your upcoming lessons. Analyze it bite by bite, breaking it down into many simple steps. And then teach the new concept one step at a time. It's a skill that takes practice, but you'll see success the first time you attempt it with your students. Once you learn to teach this way, you'll never go back. And even if you are already teaching this way, no one has yet perfected it!

Done!

Feed me the content, bite by bite
And my success, you'll certainly incite!

20-Day Reality Check

Following is a simple survey for you to complete based on all topics we have discussed since the previous 20-Day Reality Check. Your assignment today is simply to complete the survey. For each statement, write "Yes" or "No" in the right-hand column.

Survey

1	I have sent a note to parents telling of what we are accomplishing in class.	
2	I now provide frequent stretch breaks for my students.	
3	I have made it clear to my students that I care about each of them and that I am available to them if they need to talk about anything.	
4	I have learned about each of my students' heroes, and I use that information to help me better understand each student.	
5	I have left my comfort zone and improved in at least one area of my teaching.	
6	I teach vocabulary in effective ways, as opposed to expecting my students to memorize lists of words and definitions.	
7	I use the list from Day 53 in determining whether problems in my classroom are student or teacher related.	
8	I make a daily effort to speak in a calm, controlled voice.	
9	I have begun sending students to the office for positive reasons.	
10	There is a "Teacher Feature" displayed in my classroom.	
11	I have written a short note to each student, telling of an attribute I admire in him or her.	
12	I have begun posting pictures of my students in my classroom.	
13	I have begun teaching new concepts in smaller bites.	

What I Learned/What I'll Do Differently

Based on yesterday's survey results, take a few minutes to list what you have learned, what you may have already known but needed to be reminded of, what you've noticed about your students, what you will attempt to do differently in your teaching from this point forward.

_____

_____

_____

_____

_____

_____

_____

_____

_____

_____

_____

_____

_____

_____

_____

_____

_____

_____

_____

_____

_____

_____

_____

_____

_____

_____

DAY 61

Think About It

It has often been said, and most principals will agree, that 90 percent of all discipline referrals comes from less than 10 percent of all teachers. Most principals can accurately predict which teachers will send the most students to the office NEXT year! They know that the same teachers are the ones who constantly refer students to the office because of discipline problems. This is not to say that the remaining 90 percent of teachers never send students to the office, but it is a rare occurrence and thus taken seriously by the administrator. You see, when you often send students to the office for negative reasons, the message you are giving the students is that you can't handle them. Not a good message to send.

On Day 55, we encouraged you to send students to the office for positive reasons. And now we have a trick for you—a way of, technically speaking, never sending a student to the office for negative reasons!

Do It

Tell your students, "I just want you to know that if you ever do anything wrong, and you might, you don't have to worry about my sending you to the office." Students will cheer at this news. Then say, "Now, you might send yourself . . ." Say this very calmly and pleasantly and explain that the office has a few rules, and the policy is that if a student ever breaks one of those rules, they technically send themselves to the office. For instance, maybe there is a school policy that states that any physical altercations must be reported to administration. So explain this to the students and then say, "But if you ever get into a fight and send yourself to the office, I'll go ahead and fill out the paperwork for you." That's it. And that way, you never send a student to the office. Rather, by their actions, they send themselves. That's correct—the STUDENTS take responsibility for their actions. But the key to the success of this technique is that the reasons students can "send themselves to the office" are few, so it is RARE that a student ever leaves your classroom and goes to the office for something negative.

Done!

In the classrooms of teachers who choose to handle discipline problems on their own Discipline problems are fewer, more minor, and rarely become full-blown!

So Busy, I'm Dizzy!

Think About It

Keep Me Busy
Busy, busy, you keep me so busy
So much so, it makes me dizzy
Moving from one thing right to another
No time to think of anything other
Than the work I'm busy doing
Misbehavior has no time for brewing
Working, working all day long
No time for doing anything wrong
Questioning, answering, discovering, learning
There's an upward trend to the grades I'm earning
You keep me so busy and so engaged
I never have time to misbehave
Before I know it, the day is done
Learning, in your class, is really quite fun![4]

Do It

There's no secret here. In the classrooms of effective teachers, students are intentionally kept so busy that they can't find time to misbehave. These teachers plan short, quick, engaging activities (in all grade levels and subject areas) for students on a daily basis. Also, their transitions from one activity to the next are structured and quick and smooth.

Today, plan one lesson this way. Plan for student engagement, plan short, quick activities, and plan how you will move quickly from one activity to the next. Do not allow for any time when any student will have nothing to do. Literally plan for every second of the lesson. (This may sound time-consuming, but it's actually easier and more fun to plan this way. And it's certainly more fun to teach this way. And it's absolutely more fun for the students to learn this way!) Then, hold on for a fun ride! Students LOVE this type of learning. The key is to keep them so busy, it makes them dizzy!

Done!

Keep your students so engaged and active that they won't find time for behavior that's distractive!

---

[4]Breaux, *101 Poems for Teachers*, 2010. Larchmont, NY: Eye On Education.

Think About It

Students get "busted" all the time, and far too often for negative reasons. We are not suggesting that you should ignore all misbehavior from your students. We are, however, suggesting that you begin making an effort to begin busting students for behaving. In other words, turn "gotcha" into a good word in your classroom. When you begin employing the strategy of "Gotcha for doing good" as opposed "Gotcha for doing bad," the entire atmosphere in your classroom changes.

Do It

For the next five days, we will walk you through a simple exercise that will turn even the most positive of classrooms into even more positive classrooms. And, if your classroom atmosphere is a bit negative, that will change greatly with this simple exercise over the next few days. We guarantee good results. You simply cannot lose when you begin to bust your students for behaving!

Today's activity is for you to simply list the names of sixteen students—eight who typically get busted for misbehaving in your class, and eight who never get busted for misbehaving in your class. You'll be using that list for the next four days, so hold onto it. And be prepared, tomorrow, to begin busting students for good behavior.

Done!

I thought that I was busted
And it turns out that busted I was
But you busted me for behaving well
Something no one else ever does
You caught me doing something good
And you thanked me and praised me and smiled
What a clever way for an ingenious teacher
To "bust" a not-so-perfect child!
Thus proud I am now and better I'll be now
I'll get busted more often, just watch and see now!

Busted for Behaving, Part 2

Today, we would like you to take your list from yesterday and pick two students from that list who typically get busted for behaving badly and two who never get busted for behaving badly. At some time during the day today, we want you to "catch" each of those students doing something good. Then, simply notice it and praise them for it. Thank them for their good behavior. Also, pick at random a student who is not on the list, and bust him or her for behaving also. This means you will "bust" five students for behaving today. Next to all five numbers that follow, tell what you did and write a brief description of the reaction of each student.

We would like to remind you that some students don't respond favorably to being singled out in front of their peers, even if the reason for being singled out is a good one. By now, you know who those students are. So if any of the students you "bust" today fall into that category, then take care to "bust" them privately.

DAY 65

Student 1 _____

_____

_____

_____

Student 2 _____

_____

_____

_____

Student 3 _____

_____

_____

_____

Student 4 _____

_____

_____

_____

Student 5 _____

_____

_____

_____

Busted for Behaving, Part 3

Today, we would like you to take your list and pick two more students who typically get busted for behaving badly and two who never get busted for behaving badly. At some time during the day today, we want you to "catch" each of those students doing something good. Then, simply notice it and praise them for it. Thank them for their good behavior. Also, pick at random a student who is not on the list, and bust him or her for behaving also. This means you will "bust" five students for behaving today. Next to all five numbers that follow, tell what you did and write a brief description of the reaction of each student.

Again, we remind you that some students may need to be "busted" privately.

Student 1 _____

_____

_____

_____

Student 2 _____

_____

_____

_____

Student 3 _____

_____

_____

_____

Student 4 _____

_____

_____

_____

Student 5 _____

_____

_____

_____

Busted for Behaving, Part 4

Today, we would like for you to take your list and pick two more students who typically get busted for behaving badly and two who never get busted for behaving badly. At some time during the day today, we want you to "catch" each of those students doing something good. Then, simply notice it and praise them for it. Thank them for the good behavior. Also, pick at random a student who is not on the list, and bust him or her for behaving also. This means you will "bust" five students for behaving today. Next to all five numbers that follow, tell what you did and write a brief description of the reaction of each student.

Again, we remind you that some students may need to be "busted" privately.

Student 1 _____

_____

_____

_____

Student 2 _____

_____

_____

_____

Student 3 _____

_____

_____

_____

Student 4 _____

_____

_____

_____

Student 5 _____

_____

_____

_____

Busted for Behaving, Part 5

Today, we would like for you to take your list and pick the remaining two students who typically get busted for behaving badly and the remaining two who never get busted for behaving badly. At some time during the day today, we want you to "catch" each of those students doing something good. Then, simply notice it and praise them for it. Thank them for their good behavior. Also, pick at random a student who is not on the list, and bust him or her for behaving also. This means you will "bust" five students for behaving today. Next to all five numbers that follow, tell what you did and write a brief description of the reaction of each student.

Again, we remind you that some students may need to be "busted" privately.

Student 1 _____

_____

_____

_____

Student 2 _____

_____

_____

_____

Student 3 _____

_____

_____

_____

Student 4 _____

_____

_____

_____

Student 5 _____

_____

_____

_____

No Lagging in Bragging

Think About It

We hate to sound nagging, but you're lagging in bragging
Bragging about us to others
You see, we're just kids, and we need for you, teacher,
To brag to our fathers and mothers
And to brag to your friends and to anyone else
You can think of to brag, brag about us
And then when you do, our wish will come true
That you're proud of us and never doubt us!

Do It

Nothing does a better job of getting students on your side than to brag about them to others. But you can't just brag about them. You have to TELL them that you bragged about them. Whether you actually go out and brag about them to others is not really the point, but we hope that you do. What's important is that they THINK that you do. Here are a few examples of ways to tell your students you brag about them. Try at least one of them today:

♦ Just yesterday, at the faculty meeting, I was bragging about how your writing is improving so much.
♦ I told my husband last night how lucky I was to have such wonderful students to teach.
♦ A friend of mine who teaches at another school was telling me how her students have trouble getting along with one another, and I told her I was so glad my students work so hard at getting along with each other.
♦ Do you mind if I tell the principal today how much better you are all getting at following directions?
♦ I brag about this class all the time to my friends!

Done!

Tell your students, tell them often, that you're proud of them and then say why.
When you do this, the hardest of students, you'll soften. So go ahead, give it a try!

A Sticker for a Kicker

Think About It

Students LOVE stickers. And not just the elementary students! We know a principal who puts stickers on his teachers' hands when he observes exceptional lessons. Not only do the teachers love receiving the stickers, but most wear their stickers proudly all day long.

It is human nature to appreciate being recognized for a job well done. And stickers are fun ways of showing students you recognize their efforts. On an added note, they're inexpensive!

Do It

Regardless of the age level you teach, go out and get some stickers. Then, begin to give them out on a daily basis and enjoy the reactions from your students. The following are a few examples of reasons to give students stickers:

♦ Give a Happy Birthday sticker.
♦ Give a sticker that says "Thank You" when a student does something nice for you or another.
♦ Give a sticker when a student makes a good grade on an assignment.
♦ Give a sticker when a student improves behaviorally or academically.
♦ Give a sticker with a smiley face if a student looks like he or she could use some cheer.
♦ Send a sticker home to a student who is ill.
♦ Give a sticker to a student who returns to school after an absence.
♦ Give a sticker for completed homework assignments.

From today forward, get into the habit of giving a few stickers to students every day. If you're already giving stickers to students, then find yet another reason, possibly one we've already listed, for giving even more.

Done!

Give students stickers for jobs well done
They're easy to give, inexpensive, and fun
They say to your students, "You're special, you are!"
For everyone appreciates a sticky gold star!

Enthusiastic Is Fantastic

Think About It

Enthusiasm is contagious, in the classroom and in life. It is not a coincidence that effective teachers are enthusiastic teachers. Is enthusiasm enough? Of course not. You also need effective planning, instruction, and management skills, all of which we address in this book. But all the content knowledge in the world will get you nowhere if the students don't believe you love what you are teaching. That is the key: You must appear to love every minute of every day that you are teaching! Students have to be convinced that you are crazy about your content and that you are crazy about them. You must become their biggest cheerleader and their most skilled coach. You must teach with passion and energy.

Well, what if that's just not your personality? Then you are going to have to fake it if you are going to be effective. If your personality is a little dullsville, you are going to have to spice it up. The old saying, "Fake it 'til you make it" might just apply to you. The more enthusiastic you pretend to be, the more enthusiastic you will become.

Do It

Teaching is intense, because we, as teachers, are actors on a stage every minute of every day that we are teaching. And yes, teaching does involve acting. So sometimes you have to ACT enthusiastic, even and especially on those days when you are not feeling enthusiastic.

So your task today is to begin practicing your acting skills. Teach like you are on fire! Pretend that whatever you are teaching is the most important thing in the world and that you absolutely LOVE teaching it. Tell your students you've got a really exciting lesson for them today. And then teach that lesson as though it is every bit as exciting as you promised it was. Light your own spark, and yours will ignite theirs!

Done!

If you appear that you like what you're doing, and you appear to also like me
I'll be more likely to buy into what you're teaching, and a much better learner I'll be.

Don't Neglect to Earn Respect

Think About It

A struggling teacher recently said to us, "You know, teaching is not a popularity contest. I don't care if the students like me, as long as they learn from me." Oh, but we wholeheartedly disagree. We disagree because of this simple fact: Teaching is a popularity contest! It's a popularity contest with the students. If students don't like you, they won't want to learn from you. So how do you get students to like you? Do you do this by just acting like their friend and letting them do anything they want to do? Absolutely not. You get students to like you by:

- Treating each with respect and dignity
- Being fair and consistent with them
- Holding them accountable, but always in a dignified manner
- Convincing them that you like THEM
- Engaging them in meaningful activities
- Working them hard yet helping to ensure success for each
- Expressing belief in each
- Teaching with passion and enthusiasm
- Maintaining your composure and acting professionally at all costs

Teachers who do these things are popular with (and respected by) their students. And if you're popular with your students, you're automatically popular with their parents!

Do It

Today's activity is to look at the list and determine which of these you are doing and which, if any, you are not doing. If you're doing all of them, you are on the right track. If you're not, then you can easily change that. Start today to improve in at least one area.

Done!

Any effective teacher can attest
That teaching is a popularity contest
Getting students to like us is our quest
For when they do, they give us their best!

The Scoop on Groups

Think About It

Much research has been conducted and countless books have been written on the effectiveness of having students work cooperatively. Results continue to show that students who engage in cooperative learning activities enjoy improved problem-solving skills, social skills, and academic achievement, to name a few. Yet many teachers still avoid having their students work in groups for fear of students arguing, noise levels getting out of control, some students allowing others to do all of the work, among other things. These are management issues, not cooperative learning issues. In true cooperative learning, each student in the group is assigned a specific job, activities are highly structured, appropriate behavior is taught and practiced, noise levels are under control, and students are working cooperatively to accomplish a common goal. Plus, students love it when they get to interact with their peers. Even your most introverted of students may surprise you. It's a beautiful thing!

Do It

Ask yourself the following questions: Do I allow my students to work cooperatively? If not, why not? What are my biggest fears about cooperative grouping? If I am allowing students to work cooperatively, what, if any, problems are they experiencing?

We are true advocates of allowing students to work cooperatively. But we cannot, in one page, say all we would like to say on the subject. We are simply asking you to consider implementing some type of cooperative grouping in your classroom and to begin to familiarize yourself with the concept. The best way to do that is to connect with a teacher who is using it successfully.

Thus, today's activity is to speak with a fellow teacher who is having success with cooperative grouping. Get one or two ideas, and then give it a try. If you're already using cooperative grouping, we encourage you to speak with a coworker and possibly get a new idea. That's it. We believe that if you try it, you'll like it and will be more likely to continue it. But please do not make the mistake of just randomly placing students in groups and expecting them to work together. That approach will fail every time.

Done!

When people work together
There's no storm they can't weather
So teach your students to work cooperatively
And improved learning and behavior, you're sure to see!

DAY 73

Fake a Mistake

Think About It

On Days 29 through 31, we discussed mistakes, encouraging you to become more comfortable with making them and admitting them and helping your students to do the same. Today, we'll be focusing on something different. Today, we'd like to share a technique we call "Fake a Mistake," which is designed to increase student interaction. This technique works well in all grade levels and subject areas. It plays on the fact that students love to catch their teachers making mistakes. Here's how it works: Let's say that you're teaching a writing class and are trying to help students become better proof-readers. Tell your students you are going to write a paragraph on the board and they will proofread it as you write. Everyone starts the activity with their thumbs up. As soon as they catch you making a mistake, they put their thumbs down. Of course, as soon as you see thumbs down, you stop and ask, "Did I make a mistake?" and then you allow them to tell you how to correct it. The key is that everyone's thumbs either have to remain up or down, so you are increasing the likelihood that they are paying attention and actively partici-pating. You are also allowing them to do one of their favorite things—correct their teacher's mistakes!

Do It

Take your own subject area and adapt the technique we just shared to one activity today. Following the activity, write one sentence about what you noticed for each of the following areas:

Student attention: _____

_____

Student engagement: _____

_____

Student enjoyment: _____

_____

Done!

Students do a double take
When they think that their teacher has made a mistake
So fake a mistake for learning's sake,
And watch your students have fun and stay awake!

Think About It

So often, a student misbehaves, we become upset with the student, we warn or punish him, and then we wait until the next time it happens. And there usually is a next time. Students resent being singled out and embarrassed in front of their peers. When we handle problems this way, the misbehavior often stops for a time. But it usually resurfaces.

We encourage you to use a different approach—one that actually works. We call it the *private practice session*. When a student misbehaves or does not follow one of your procedures, you pretend to assume that he simply "forgot" the procedure or the appropriate behavior. Then you offer your own time to practice with him so that he does not forget again. Instead of being mad at him, you are sympathizing with him and helping him not to forget again. This practice session is quick, and it is always done in private—just you and the student.

Do It

Let's say that a student is exhibiting the one behavior that rattles teachers more than any other—constantly talking out of turn. Talk to the student privately and say, "I see that you keep forgetting the procedure about raising your hand before speaking. I understand how easy it is to forget, because I sometimes forget things too. And I know how embarrassing it is to forget so often in front of your friends. So here's what I'm willing to do for you. Don't thank me now; I'm happy to do this in order to help you. I'm going to give you my recess today and practice with you. See you at recess." (Say it all with a smile on your face.) Then, at recess, ask him to show you what he will do the next time he wants to speak. When he raises his hand, simply say, "Great! Do you need more practice or do you think you have it?" Expect for him to say, "I'm good." And send him on his way. It takes all of 30 seconds. Even if you don't have a scheduled recess, the technique only takes 30 seconds so you can do it any time, as long as it is done in private. That's it. The student is not punished; he thinks that you think he is just forgetting and so you are offering your own time to practice with him, and there is no power struggle. These are the reasons it works amazingly well!

Done!

If, after implementing this technique, the student repeats the misbehavior, simply have another private practice session. Soon, he will learn that each time he "forgets," you practice with him. Soon, his "memory" will begin to improve!

DAY 76

Think About It

Students of all ages love having fun. So do adults, hopefully. We continue to see that effective teachers make learning fun. Students also like being timed (though not during tests), as it puts a sense of urgency and importance on the activity. Today's activity helps you to do just that. We call it "One Minute to Win It." It's a simple game where students are given one minute to write three things (you may choose to make it one or two in lower grades) that they have learned today. Then, you allow them to share with the class what they have learned. The time spent allowing students to discuss what they have learned makes for wonderful review time of whatever concepts you have taught on that particular day or for a particular lesson.

Prizes do not ever have to be expensive or elaborate. Sample prizes might include:

♦ An extra point on a test
♦ A homework assignment they may choose to opt out of
♦ Stickers
♦ Free time

Please do not make the mistake of viewing any of this as elementary-type activities. Students of all ages enjoy playing games, having fun, and winning prizes.

Do It

For today, tell your students, "We are going to play a game called *One Minute to Win It*. Everyone, take out one sheet of paper and put your name on it. You will then have one minute to write three things you learned today in my class. I'll be timing you, and you have to stop when I tell you that your time is up. Then, I'll allow each of you to tell me the three things you have written on your paper. Anyone who can list three things that he or she has learned today will receive _____" (and you tell them about the prize they will win).

We feel certain that you will begin to use this activity often, as you will see how the students enjoy it and how it allows for valuable review of concepts.

Done!

Make it fun and I'll want to do it
Even though it's challenging, I'll push on through it
And place a prize at the finish line
And I'll try even harder at whatever you assign.

Pretend Not to Comprehend What They Intend

Think About It

Since we, as teachers, can easily recognize the warning signs when a student is about to misbehave, we tend to use the old "Don't you dare do that" speech a little too often. When we do this, the student denies that he was about to do anything. And if we're not able to stop a student before the misbehavior begins, we then have to deal with it after it has already happened. Still, even when we catch him in the act, he often denies that he was actually doing what we have accused him of doing! Effective teachers have a secret . . . They often *trick* a student into behaving by pretending to assume that the student was doing whatever he was doing with noble intentions. It's actually quite fun!

Do It

Try something today. When you notice a student who is preparing to do something inappropriate, be it tease another student or talk out of turn or get out of his seat just to walk around when he isn't supposed to be doing so, approach him as if you think he is doing something noble. Say something like, "Sam, I know that you must have a really important question for me because you're out of your desk when you're not supposed to be, so go ahead and sit down, and I'll be right there to answer your question. Thanks, Sam." Another example might be, "Melanie, I can tell you were on your way to help others with their work, but go ahead and be seated and I'll see if anyone needs assistance. But I really appreciate your willingness to help. Thanks." And yet another example is saying something like, "Jess, I can tell you want to put a lot of thought into your work before you actually begin, but see if you can get started now, because we don't have a lot of time left. Thanks." Remember that your tone cannot be sarcastic—this is another chance to practice your acting skills.

This simple technique has worked wonders for teachers and students. Give it a try. Start pretending!

Done!

You pretended not to have comprehended what I had intended
And you did it so well
That I actually thought that you thought I had good intentions
So I'll never tell!
And I'll never know if you ever knew that what I intended was not noble
Great strategy, teacher! So spread it around to others and let it go global!

Think About It

"Oh, so you're a teacher, huh? You finish your day around 3 p.m. and you get all those holidays and lots of time off in the summer. It must be nice!" We've all heard this. But notice that whoever says this has never been a teacher. They just don't get it! They don't understand that what makes teaching so difficult is the fact that we don't have the luxury of having one "off" minute. The students are watching us constantly, so we must be positive role models constantly. The students are learning from us constantly, so we must give 100 percent of our efforts to them every minute of every school day. Effective teaching is exhausting! It's not easy to pretend to be in control all the time, to walk around every day with a huge smile on your face, to be prepared for all the unpredictable events that will occur every day of any school year, to handle all situations professionally, to avoid the allure of negativity, and more. No, it's not easy, but it is so rewarding and worthwhile.

Do It

Your simple activity today is to get a piece of paper or an index card and write two words on it: ROLE MODEL. Then post it where you will see it every day. Maybe tape it to the top of your desk. Maybe tape it inside of a drawer that you open daily. The key is to put it in a place where you will see it EVERY DAY. We're all human, and we all need reminders. It's easy to forget that the students are watching us constantly, and thus we become way too human at times. But we really don't have that luxury—not while the students are watching.

Done!

No botching because they're watching
Not a hurtful word that anyone's heard
No gossip, no complaining, no lack of sunshine when it's raining
No giving up, no giving in, no accepting defeat when you've got to win

For you are the ultimate role model, so be what you hope they become
Your students are watching and learning from you
They dance to the beat of your drum
So be a drummer with a rhythm so true that others can set their clocks by you
And know that you're shaping the future each day
On the roads of young lives, you're paving the way!

Think About It

If you were to go into any school and ask the students, "Who are the screamers on this faculty," could the students tell you? Absolutely they could, and usually with 100 percent accuracy! It's a well-known fact that students know who the screamers are on the faculty.

The fact is that if you lose your cool, you lose control—of yourself and of the situation. You also set the example that when you get aggravated enough, it's okay to lose your cool. And that is the LAST example we ever want to set for students. We believe that it is never appropriate to yell at students. It is fine to hold them accountable when their actions warrant it, but always do so in a calm, controlled manner. (As we discussed on Day 54, the louder a student gets, the softer you must become.)

Do It

On Day 11, we asked you to make a promise to your students that, though you would hold them accountable, you would not do so by losing your cool and screaming at them. Have you held to that promise? If so, pat yourself on the back and take the day off. You have no further activity for today. If, however, you have not held to that promise, or, maybe you didn't even make the promise, please reconsider. Ask yourself why it is that you are screaming at your students, even if it's only occasionally, and then decide how you might begin working at maintaining your composure.

Done!

If you're one who's touting your power by shouting
Then power you do not possess
To be influential and tap their potential
Teach with poise, control, and finesse
When you show aggravation and vent your frustration
Then students' behaviors just worsen
So do not reveal sweat, but better yet
Just be a professional person!

DAY 79

Following is a simple survey for you to complete based on all topics we have discussed since the previous 20-Day Reality Check. Your assignment today is simply to complete the survey. For each statement, write "Yes" or "No" in the right-hand column.

Survey

1	I avoid sending students to the office for negative reasons.	
2	I keep my students so busy and engaged that they have trouble finding time to misbehave.	
3	I have begun "busting" students for behaving.	
4	I tell my students that I brag about them to others.	
5	I have begun giving students stickers for positive achievements.	
6	I have been practicing my acting skills and appearing even more enthusiastic in my teaching.	
7	I work diligently to earn the respect of my students.	
8	I provide opportunities for students to work cooperatively in groups.	
9	I have begun playing the "Fake a Mistake" game with my students.	
10	I am using the "Private Practice Session" technique from Day 75.	
11	I have tried the "Minute to Win It" game with my students.	
12	I pretend to assume that my students have nobler intentions than they sometimes do.	
13	I have a way of reminding myself daily that I am a role model for my students, and I strive to be the most positive role model I can be.	
14	I consider self-control one of my most important personal goals.	

What I Learned/What I'll Do Differently

Based on yesterday's survey results, take a few minutes to list what you have learned, what you may have already known but needed to be reminded of, what you've noticed about your students, what you will attempt to do differently in your teaching from this point forward.

I Believe You Can Achieve

Think About It

If I do not believe that I can achieve
Then I won't, for reality's what I perceive
But if I believe with all of my might
That achieving a goal is within my sight
Then chances improve and mountains I'll move
So help me believe, and then watch me achieve!

Do It

Teachers know that students are more likely to achieve whatever it is they believe they can achieve! But sometimes students need a little help believing they can achieve. The simple words, "I believe in you" or "I believe you can do this" are very powerful. As teachers, sometimes we actually do believe that a student can achieve, but we forget to express that belief. Or, we mean well, but we give our beliefs a negative slant by saying things such as "You can do better than this" or "You're capable of doing better work" or "I don't know why you can't see your own potential."

Be careful, of course, to be realistic in expressing your belief. For instance, you would not want to tell a student who is struggling to write a complete sentence that you believe he can write an essay today.

For today's activity, use the following phrases (or similar ones) with several students who are having trouble believing in themselves:

- ◆ I've noticed you're getting much better at _____ .

- ◆ Have you noticed how much better you're doing with _____ ?

- ◆ I'm proud of you for _____ and I really believe in you. You're showing so much improvement.

- ◆ You can do this. I know you can! And I'll help you to prove that to yourself.

Done!

Expressing belief in your students can only help them to try harder, to do better, and to believe in themselves.

Think About It

Whether My Students Pass or Fail
He did not pass my test—because he didn't study
And so I took my red pen and made his paper bloody
And then I started thinking about what I was doing
What in the world was I trying to prove? What point was I pursuing?
If studying determined his grade, what had I really taught?
If studying was the only way to pass, in class, no learning was wrought
Yes, studying is important, but teaching should mean more
If I'm really teaching every day, it should affect his score
Studying might make the difference between and A and a B
But whether my students pass or fail really depends on me![5]

We've all heard a teacher say, "Well, of course he didn't pass the test. He admitted he didn't study." Is this teacher basing a student's grade solely on what he does or does not do at home? Though we are not suggesting that studying is unimportant, we ARE suggesting that the majority of students' grades should be indicative of what they do or don't learn from us, their teachers, in our classrooms.

Do It

Teachers who test what they teach, in the same way that they have taught it, do not face the dilemma of students not passing tests due to lack of studying. Do students perform better on tests if they study and practice on their own? Yes. But they don't fail tests based solely on their study habits. As teachers, we continually assess students' understanding while we are teaching. If a student does not understand a concept, we remediate before the test, thus increasing his or her chances of success. And when a student fails a test, we don't rush to place blame on him but rather we look at what we might be able to do differently to help him succeed.

Today's activity simply involves answering this question: Do students ever fail to pass tests in my class based on their study habits?

Done!

Teach what you will test and then test what you have taught. Will they all make As? No. But all students can achieve and succeed in the hands of great teachers!

---

[5]Breaux and Whitaker, *Seven Simple Secrets*, 2006. Larchmont, NY: Eye On Education.

Pry for Why[6]

Think About It

It has often been said that if we knew the *reasons* behind the misbehavior of our students, instead of being angry, we'd usually be heartbroken. Oftentimes when a student misbehaves, we dole out a punishment, and we dare the student to misbehave again. But we forget the most important piece—finding out "why."

Do It

We conducted an experiment with teachers and taught them the *Pry for Why* technique. This technique involves exactly what it implies. When a student misbehaves, maintain your composure and talk to him calmly. Ask why he acted in that way. Do this in a very sincere manner, and do it privately. Keep your frustrations out of it. If he mutters the famous student comeback, "I don't know," then simply say, "Well, think about it and we'll talk again a little later. You probably just need some time to figure it out." And always come back later and talk to him again. Usually, you will learn that there is a definite reason for the misbehavior.

During our experiment, teachers were amazed at the things they learned by simply prying for why. And, more often than not, they were heartbroken over what they heard.

Try it. When a student misbehaves, simply pry for why. That does not mean that you will excuse the student for the misbehavior, but chances are good that you will deal with the misbehavior much more effectively.

Done!

When a student misbehaves, there is usually a reason. And usually the misbehavior is a cry for help. When you know the reason, you can better provide help and deal with the misbehavior in a way that will foster better behavior in the future. The *Pry for Why* technique is an easy, stress-free, effective way of doing this. So we challenge you to pry for why!

---

[6]Breaux and Whitaker, *50 Ways to Improve Student Behavior*, 2010. Larchmont, NY: Eye On Education.

What They Hide Inside

Think About It

Yesterday, we suggested prying for why when a student misbehaves. Knowing why a student does what he does helps us to more effectively deal with the student. But oh the things they hide inside! Sometimes we find out and sometimes we don't. Many of our students come to us from wonderful homes with supportive parents. Many do not. But all of them, by the nature of being human, struggle from time to time. Some, obviously, struggle more than others. We teach some students who don't know who their parents are, who don't have homes, who witness horrors we cannot begin to imagine on a daily basis, who are malnourished, who are misguided, who are afraid. And the list goes on.

How can we expect some of our students to be, in any way, motivated to learn what we have to teach them? That's the magic of teachers! Teachers understand that students, regardless of their experiences and sometimes because of them, NEED to have a safe haven at school, to feel loved, respected, and appreciated, to achieve and taste success. All children need this! All children need teachers!

Do It

Think about the fact that, today, there are things in your life that worry you, that upset you, that bother you, that scare you. Hopefully, these issues do not consume you, but they are real and they are present. Now consider the fact that you are an adult, better equipped to deal with life's difficulties than are children.

And now take a good look at every one of your students and know that all of them face difficulties, struggles, and fears—most of which they hide inside. Just knowing this will change the way you approach them, the way you teach them, and the way you deal with their behavior, both good and bad.

Done!

Treat each student as if he needs you, because need you, all students do
And when looking back at their greatest heroes, they'll all remember YOU!

DAY 86

Think About It

If someone were to ask any student you have ever taught, "Who is the most positive teacher you have ever had?," would he or she name you?

Do It

If you do not believe that your students would name you if asked about the most positive teacher they have ever had, you can change that today with the students you are teaching this year. The good news is that students will believe you're a changed person if you exhibit a positive change in your behavior for a few days in a row. For instance, if you tend to be a little negative and you decide to act positive for three or four days, students will buy into it and believe that you have really changed. That's because they are children and they are trusting. Adults, however, are not nearly as trusting. Go ahead and try convincing a spouse or a family member that you are suddenly more positive. They'll become downright suspicious, saying things like, "What's wrong?" or "What do you want?" Exhibit this same behavior, consistently, for six months. They'll continue to be suspicious!

Well, thankfully, students will believe that you are a *new person* if you exhibit positive behavior, consistently, for just a few days. And who of us doesn't want our students to remember us as the most positive teacher they ever had? So fake it if you must, but begin, today, to be a model of optimism in your classroom. It's actually quite fun. And, of course, students respond favorably to positive teachers. (See Day 97.)

Done!

Who is the happiest teacher—the most professional in my school?
If I can't honestly say it's me, then surely I'm a fool
For any effective teacher knows, certainly, one thing
Students want happy teachers more than anything
So I'm starting to appear happy today, and when looking back, my students will say,
"Of all the teachers I ever knew, the happiest one of all was you!"

Clean Your Room

Think About It

"Clean your room!" is a phrase often spoken by parents to their children. Today, however, we address you, our fellow teachers, when we say, "Clean your room." We continue to notice that messy classrooms are often chaotic ones. We also notice that when the teacher is disorganized, the students are disorganized.

We are not suggesting that just because your classroom is neat and orderly, you will be an effective teacher. But we do notice that great teachers are well organized, they know how to find whatever it is they need in their classrooms, they model organization for their students, and they help their students to become better organized. Their orderly environments, we believe, foster more orderly behavior. This does not mean that they are obsessively neat and overly organized. But their classrooms are never messy places.

When your classroom is neat and organized, it portrays the following messages to students:

♦ This is an orderly, safe place.
♦ I take pride in our classroom.
♦ I care enough about you to provide you with a neat environment.
♦ I take pride in myself and in my teaching.

Let's face it—it's important to be able to find what you need when you need it. It's important that aisles are free of clutter to promote safety and to allow you to move freely from one student to the next. It's important that students see *order* and not *chaos* in the environment that you create for them.

Do It

Take a look at your classroom environment. If it's a little (or a lot) disheveled, clean it up! It's worth the time, it's worth the effort, it makes you appear more professional, it helps you to be more productive, and it shows the students (and anyone else who walks into your classroom) all that we listed earlier. There simply is no downside to having an orderly environment!

Done!

When everything is everywhere, you simply can't find anything there
But put each item in its place, and your classroom will be a more productive space!

DAY 87

Think About It

Back in 1979, a study conducted on Harvard MBA students revealed that only 3 percent had clear, written goals for their futures. Thirteen percent had goals, but those goals were not written. And 84 percent had no specific goals at all. Long story short: Only ten years later, the 13 percent who had unwritten goals were earning, on average, twice as much as the 84 percent who had no goals. And the 3 percent who had clear, written goals were earning ten times more than the other 97 percent combined![7]

This is only one of many compelling studies showing the importance of having clear, written goals. When you know where you're going, your chances of getting there increase exponentially! So why is it that so few people actually have written goals for their lives with plans for how they will achieve those goals?

If you were to walk into almost any classroom and ask the students, "Who among you has written goals telling what you want to accomplish this year, next year, or further into your future?" you will see very few, if any, raised hands. We, as teachers, can turn that around!

Do It

Have a brief discussion with your students today and find out how many, if any of them, actually have goals for their future. Talk to them about the importance of having dreams and setting goals and having plans to help them achieve those goals. Explain to them that people who have written goals achieve and succeed much more than those who don't. And tell them that tomorrow, you will help each of them to come up with specific, written goals. Share your own enthusiasm for this activity. Remember, ALL students have dreams, and, despite their outward behavior at times, they ALL want to succeed in life! Every day, you, their teacher, are helping them to realize those dreams.

Done!

If you're headed nowhere, you'll arrive nowhere, potentially. . . . But when you know just where you're going, your chances of getting there increase exponentially!

---

[7]McCormack, *What They Don't Teach You at Harvard Business School*, 1986. New York: Bantam.

DAY 88

Think About It

At the risk of overstating the obvious, it will probably come as no surprise that most students do not have written goals. Even those who do know their goals are often afraid to admit them, much less write them, for fear that they're being unrealistic and may fail at accomplishing these goals. This, by the way, is the same reason that so many adults do not have written goals. But, once you know the power of having written goals, it's almost impossible not to give it a try and put your goals in writing. It takes only a few minutes, and the results can be life-altering!

The real key is to imagine that you absolutely cannot fail. If you knew that, what would your goals become? This is how you will want to approach goal writing with your students.

Do It

Today, have your students write one to three goals they would like to accomplish. Have them write at least one goal they would like to accomplish this year. For very young students, you may choose to have them draw a picture of their goals. This activity should take only a few minutes.

Done!

Let your students know that you will ask each of them, tomorrow and the day after, to share at least one goal with the class. The reason for this is best explained by the following example: If you go on a diet and tell no one, there is no real pressure to lose weight. If you fail, no one knows but you. If you go on a diet and tell everyone you know, you will be more likely to succeed, knowing that others are aware of your goal. A little peer pressure can sometimes be a good thing! However, if there is one student who, for whatever reason, is adamant about not sharing his or her goals with classmates, then please don't push the issue. The real purpose of this activity is to get students thinking about having and accomplishing goals.

The Goal Post, Part 3

Today, you will simply take a few minutes to have half of your students share at least one of their goals with the class. The second half will share tomorrow. After each shares his or her goal, provide a few words of encouragement in order to help him or her begin to take steps toward that goal.

We suggest that you write at least one of each student's goals so that you have these to keep. Occasionally, refer to them and check with the students as to their progress in accomplishing these goals. This will help to encourage students to strive for success, and it will also continue to send a message that you care about each.

Students' Goals: _____

_____

_____

_____

_____

_____

_____

_____

_____

_____

_____

_____

_____

_____

_____

_____

_____

_____

_____

_____

_____

_____

_____

_____

DAY 90

The Goal Post, Part 4

Today, you will simply take a few minutes to have the second half of your students share at least one of their goals with the class. After each shares his or her goal, remember to provide a few words of encouragement in order to help him or her begin to take steps toward that goal.

Students' Goals: _____

_____

_____

_____

_____

_____

_____

_____

_____

_____

_____

_____

_____

_____

_____

_____

_____

_____

_____

_____

_____

_____

_____

_____

_____

_____

Recognize the Warning Signs and Nip It in the Bud

Think About It

As teachers, we are constantly assessing student understanding. We have ways of spotting, immediately, when a student does not understand a concept. Here are a few of the warning signs we often see from students:

♦ Looks of confusion
♦ Inability to perform a task related to a new concept
♦ Questions that reveal confusion or lack of understanding
♦ Giving up on a task, sometimes pretending not to care
♦ Failure to complete a task related to a new concept
♦ Acting out with inappropriate behavior
♦ Withdrawing and refusing to participate in class

The list goes on, but the point is that there are definite warning signs pointing to lack of student understanding. We get ourselves and our students into trouble, however, when we forget to pay attention to these warning signs and nip a problem in the bud before it becomes too significant. Or we jump to conclusions, assuming a student is lazy or not trying hard enough or just does not care. We urge you to be VERY careful about jumping to any such conclusions.

Do It

Look at the previous list and add any other warning signs you may notice with your own students. Then, attempt to quickly nip problems in the bud before they become bigger. If you notice confusion on a student's face today, go to him immediately and assess his understanding. Provide some quick remediation, if necessary, and then pat yourself on the back for averting a potential problem. If a student is refusing to do his work, talk to him and find out what's going on before you admonish him for not getting busy. Do this today and every day. Nip those problems in the bud so that they never actually bloom!

Done!

There's no bloom without a bud
Without dirt, there is no mud
Without a fall, there is no thud
Without a cut, there is no blood
So nip a problem in the bud
And prevent the mud, blood, and thud!

DAY 92

Think About It

Have you ever received an award? Even if it was back in grade school, and you received an award for making good grades or exhibiting good behavior or winning a contest, can't you still remember how good it felt to hold that certificate or that trophy in your hands? Can't you remember how proud you were to bring that award home and show it to your family? Can't you remember how good it felt for your teacher and your family and your friends to be proud of you?

Hopefully, you have such a memory. If you don't, you should, because every student deserves to receive awards for jobs well done. Sadly, many don't. But you can change that today. And no, we are not asking you to go out and spend money on awards. The fact is that awards don't have to be elaborate or expensive. They just need to signify something very, very important—recognition for a job well done!

Do It

Plan a very simple awards ceremony for your entire class. You can either print the awards on your computer or make them by hand. The key is to present every student with some type of award during your ceremony. Here are a few ideas for awards: most improved, best behavior, most helpful, best attendance record, kindest, most likely to _____ (you can fill in that blank with endless possibilities), most creative, funniest, best grade point average, best attitude, and so on.

Tell them that these are your mid-year awards and let them know that there will also be an end-of-year awards day. The ceremony will take only a few minutes, but it will be so worth your time and effort. It will also show your students that you notice the good in each of them.

Done!

You certainly caught me off guard
When you presented me with an award
An award that said that I was one who was worthy of recognition
An award for me? That cannot be! At first I was filled with suspicion
But then I realized that you were right—at some things, I was good
And so I set my sights on being as good as I possibly could
Oh that precious piece of paper, that certificate of award
Just looking at it on my wall each day makes me want to work extra hard!

DAY 93

Think About It

Have you ever stopped at the supermarket on your way home from work? Can't you spot people you know are on their way home from work by the way they are dressed? You can spot men and women who are dressed professionally, and you can accurately assume that they are on their way home from a day at the office.

If you walk into a courtroom, you can pick out the attorneys because of the way they are dressed. If you walk through an airport, you can easily spot the pilots and the flight attendants. That is because the pilots and flight attendants are professionally dressed in some type of uniform. But wouldn't the pilot be just as capable if he were wearing jeans? Yes, he would, but the problem is that the passengers would not view him that way. If you walked into a school, could you immediately pick out all the teachers based on their professional attire? Not always. Does lack of professional dress make a teacher any less competent? No. But it does affect the way that that teacher's students perceive him or her, which inevitably affects the teacher's effectiveness.

The fact is that the way we dress often helps to determine how others view us. If teaching is the noblest profession of all, shouldn't all teachers dress the part? We believe they should. Does that mean that teachers should spend their meager salaries to buy expensive clothing? No. But they should not dress like their students. You don't need to buy fancy clothing in order to look like a professional.

Do It

Ask yourself a simple question today: "If a stranger were to meet me on my way to school, would he know that I am some type of professional based on the way I am dressed?"

Done!

I dressed like my students, because I thought they'd think I was cool
You wouldn't have known I was a professional if you'd spotted me at school
You see, I did not realize that my students did not take me seriously
But the day I dressed like a professional, their attitudes changed, mysteriously
And so, today, I dress and act just like a professional does
And my students think that I'm one of the coolest teachers there ever was!

Do You Teach the Way You Were Taught?

Think About It

We often hear and see that some teachers tend to teach the way they were taught. We even hear some teachers saying, "Well, that's the way I learned it and it worked for me." And though we do not believe that all the techniques of 10, 20, 30, or more years ago are ineffective, we DO believe that teachers cannot expect to be effective today if they are simply teaching the same ways they were taught many years ago.

Imagine a doctor saying, "That's how I was treated when I had cancer 15 years ago, so that's how I'll treat my patients today." Imagine a technology engineer saying, "This is the computer I used ten years ago, and it worked for me then so it should work for everyone now!" You see, the world continues to change. We continue to discover new and better ways of achieving results. In teaching, we know so much more today than we did even five years ago, and we continue to discover more effective ways of preparing our students to function in today's world, not yesterday's. That's not to say that we should throw out everything from the past. Rather, we should continue to learn and grow in our profession so that we can better determine what works today and what does not when it comes to teaching our students.

We discussed Round Robin Reading on Day 50. No one actually learned to read using this technique. We know this now, yet some teachers continue to use it because that's the way they were taught! And that is not a good enough reason to continue doing something that simply does not work.

Do It

Look at each lesson you teach today, and ask yourself why you are teaching what you are teaching in the specific way that you are teaching it. If you find that you don't really know why you're teaching a certain lesson in a certain way, then chances are good that you are teaching the way you were taught simply because it's the way you were taught. Start today to teach everything in a certain way for a very specific reason—that it's the most effective way to teach and for your students to learn. (You may want to refer to Days 49 through 52.)

Done!

Think about why you teach as you do
And examine the reasons, and think it all through
And learn and grow so that soon you will know
What to keep from the old days and what you should throw!

Think About It

New teachers consistently receive a lot of advice from well-meaning veteran teachers. One typical piece of advice is, "Whatever you do, stay away from the teachers' lounge!" Have you heard it? Why is it that so many teachers warn others to stay away from the lounge? The reason is simple. Occasionally, well, okay, maybe more than occasionally, negative teachers have been known to lurk there. They moan and complain and make everyone else so uncomfortable that the positive teachers often end up avoiding the lounge altogether. So the negative people win! They get to have dibs on the coffee and occasional desserts and they get to have a place to put their feet up, at the expense of the positive teachers who have EARNED that coffee or those desserts. We have a solution . . .

Do It

Starting today, enlist the support of a few positive coworkers and agree to go to the lounge every time you get a break, even if it's just for five minutes. Walk into the lounge with huge smiles on your faces. Be more positive than you have ever been. Whenever a negative coworker speaks ill of a student (and they will!), simply reply with, "I love that kid." We don't care if you don't even know that kid. Pretend to know him and love him. Do this every day, and have fun watching the looks of confusion on the faces of all the pessimists as you and your positive coworkers discuss your love of teaching and brag about all of your wonderful students. Soon enough, they will become so uncomfortable that they'll begin avoiding the lounge. We believe that it's time to take our lounges back!

Done!

We go to the lounge when we need a break
And we wear big smiles even if they're fake
And of students and others, we only speak well
Harsh words and gossip, we never tell
And it makes all the pessimists ill at ease
For we take away their opportunities to seize
Even one second to speak ill of another
To criticize a student or administrator or mother
And so they leave with their heads hanging low
And, to the lounge, no longer do they go
For the lounge now wears a happy face
Because our positive attitudes pervade the place!

A Smile Is in Style

Think About It

On Day 1, we talked about the fact that students need happy adults in their lives. You simply cannot help students by being yet another negative influence in their lives. This, of course, is not earth-shattering news. But we all need to remind ourselves, from time to time, that our attitudes are contagious. Show us a negative teacher, and we'll show you a classroom with many problems. Is it always easy to appear upbeat? No. Is it necessary? Only if you want to be effective. Are effective teachers always happy and upbeat? No, they just appear so!

We know a teacher—one of the most effective educators we've ever encountered—who always appears happy. Not surprisingly, she has no discipline problems. BUT, she teaches some of the most challenging students we've ever encountered, both behaviorally and academically! We asked about why she smiles all the time, and she answered, "I smile all the time because it is virtually impossible for a student to misbehave when you're smiling at him or her!" She's right. Try it, consistently, and you'll soon agree. Now, does this teacher smile when a student is doing something inappropriate? No, she does not. She becomes very serious and speaks to the student very softly, and then she smiles at everyone else and continues teaching.

Do It

It is a scientific fact that when you smile, your brain releases endorphins, which are your body's natural pain killers. You immediately begin to feel better. If you don't believe us, then try this: Smile and try to get depressed while you are smiling. Keep smiling and try to get depressed. You simply can't do it! Smiling is also contagious. When someone is smiling at you, it is difficult not to smile back. Not impossible, but difficult. Happy teachers have happy classrooms. And, sadly, for some of your students, yours may be the only smile they see all day. Knowing that, you can probably guess what your simple assignment is today. Start smiling! You won't need any further instructions because you'll see the results for yourself.

Done!

Smile, smile, smile at me
And happier, happier we both will be
For happy students misbehave a lot less
And happy teachers have much less stress!

Are You Quite All Right?[8]

Think About It

"Are you all right?" These four words say "I care about you." What feels better, for any of us, than to know that someone cares about us? What student wouldn't behave better if he felt his teacher cared about him? Conversely, what student would be motivated to behave well in the classroom of a teacher who didn't care?

Do It

We call it the "Are you all right?" technique and it is based on the simple premise that students who believe you care about them are much more apt to behave better. Here's what you do: The next time a student misbehaves, take him aside and ask, "Are you all right?" You may be surprised at the look on the student's face. Most always, the student will answer, "Yes." Then say, "Well the reason I'm asking is that the way you were behaving was inappropriate and not at all like you." (Okay, so maybe you're stretching the truth a little, as the behavior was very typical of that student, but we think you can see where we're going with this.) Continue by saying, "So I knew for you to be acting that way, something must be bothering you. And I just wanted you to know that I'm here for you if you want to talk about it." That's it!

Did you deal with the misbehavior? Yes. You made it clear that the behavior was inappropriate. Will the student's behavior improve? Almost always! Please note that what you did *not* do was very important. You did not dare him to do it again, you did not act personally offended, you did not threaten him, and you did not belittle him. You simply expressed caring and concern about his inappropriate behavior. The "Are you all right?" technique will surprise you with its effectiveness if you use it appropriately.

Done!

The fact that some students assume that their teachers don't care about them often leads to misbehavior, indignant attitudes, disrespect, apathy, and lack of motivation. The fact that some teachers know how to show their students they care often leads to good behavior, positive attitudes, respect, interest, and motivation. Which would you prefer?

---

[8]Breaux and Whitaker, *50 Ways to Improve Student Behavior*, 2010. Larchmont, NY: Eye On Education.

Think About It

Think back to your days as a student. Do you remember how good it felt and how proud you were when one of your teachers attended your basketball game or your football game or your band concert or your school's talent show? Better yet, do you remember your teacher saying to you, the next day, "That was a great game last night!" or "You were awesome on stage!"?

Seeing a teacher outside of the daily school setting is a whole different experience for students. It's like they think their teachers live in the classrooms, even at night, so they are shocked and usually overjoyed to spot their teachers doing something *normal* and being out in the world! Wow! Running into a teacher in the grocery store is an ethereal experience for a student, but seeing a teacher attend an after-school function is even more otherworldly!

Do It

We all have busy lives outside of school. But, whenever possible, attend your students' after-school functions. You can't attend them all, and you can't even attend most, but attend as many as possible. It sends a message to students, once again, that you care about them. And as we discussed yesterday and have mentioned throughout this book and can never mention enough, students who believe their teachers care about them behave better and try harder in class.

Done!

She Cheered for Me
There must be some type of crazy malfunction
For my teacher was at my after-school function
I thought that she lived in her classroom at school
Did they let her out? 'Cause it's extremely cool
That my teacher cared enough to come to the game
She cheered for me, so, for her I'll do the same![9]

DAY 99

---

[9]Breaux, *101 "Answers" for New Teachers and Their Mentors* (2nd ed.), 2011. Larchmont, NY: Eye On Education.

20-Day Reality Check

Following is a simple survey for you to complete based on all topics we have discussed since the previous 20-Day Reality Check. Your assignment today is simply to complete the survey. For each statement, write "Yes" or "No" in the right-hand column.

Survey

1	I make a special effort to express belief in all of my students.	
2	I test what I teach in class in the same way that I have taught it.	
3	I always try to pry for why when a student is misbehaving or acting withdrawn or suddenly losing interest.	
4	I remind myself that all students have their own personal struggles that can affect their behavior or performance in my classroom.	
5	My students think I am very positive.	
6	I keep my classroom neat, organized, and clutter-free.	
7	I have helped my students to write personal goals.	
8	We have discussed these goals.	
9	I look for signs warning that a student does not understand a concept, and I provide remediation so that the student does not fall behind.	
10	I have held some type of awards ceremony, acknowledging each of my students for some type of achievement.	
11	I dress professionally.	
12	I display a positive attitude in the teachers' lounge.	
13	I have used the "Are you all right?" technique.	
14	I attend after-school functions when possible.	

What I Learned/What I'll Do Differently

Based on yesterday's survey results, take a few minutes to list what you have learned, what you may have already known but needed to be reminded of, what you've noticed about your students, what you will attempt to do differently in your teaching from this point forward.

_____

_____

_____

_____

_____

_____

_____

_____

_____

_____

_____

_____

_____

_____

_____

_____

_____

_____

_____

_____

_____

_____

_____

_____

_____

_____

_____

_____

_____

_____

DAY 101

Think About It

Knowing what NOT to do in a classroom is every bit as important as knowing what TO do! We believe that most teachers do the very best they can with what they know. Teachers sometimes make mistakes that stem from not knowing what to do. So we guess . . . And sometimes we guess wrongly. Or we act out of frustration, realizing it's not appropriate but giving in to feelings of anxiety or inundation. This is a slippery slope because when you don't know what to do, it is usually better to wait, calm down, and think about an appropriate, professional way to handle the situation.

Do It

The following are examples of what NOT to do in the classroom or in the school:

♦ Do not allow students to push your buttons.
♦ If students do push your buttons, do not let them know it.
♦ Do not discipline a student in front of his or her peers.
♦ Do not get into power struggles with students.
♦ Do not raise your voice when dealing with a student.
♦ Do not forget that you are the adult in the classroom.
♦ Do not speak ill of others.
♦ Do not fall victim to the blame game.
♦ Do not expect your students to make adult-like decisions.
♦ Do not come to school unprepared—ever!
♦ Do not act in any way other than professional.
♦ Do not dress like your students.
♦ Do not act like your students.
♦ Do not forget to be consistent with your rules and procedures.
♦ Do not be afraid to admit a mistake when you have made one.
♦ Do not be afraid to ask for help when you need it.

Done!

Last, but definitely not least, never forget why you chose teaching. You chose teaching because you wanted to make a difference in the lives of students. You did not choose it because you thought it would be easy or because you thought it would make you financially wealthy or because you heard there was very little paperwork!

Risky Business

Think About It

Have you ever had a relationship, learned to play a sport, learned a new skill such as driving a car, hosted a party, expressed an opinion, helped someone in need, or gone on a vacation? All of these activities involved risk. Learning to drive was a little scary, but the outcome was going to be so very worth it, right? The simple act of expressing an opinion involves the risk that others may disagree with you. Risking love involves risking loss. Learning a new skill involves risking failure. But the fact is that people who don't risk are people who never accomplish! All great leaders are risk takers. All great teachers are risk takers. All successful people are risk takers.

We know that positive risk taking promotes personal growth, builds confidence, builds self-esteem, builds courage, and arouses creativity and passion. Don't we want our students to possess all of those traits? If so, then we have to create a classroom climate that is conducive to risk taking.

Do It

The following are a few ways to help your students become more comfortable with positive risk taking:

♦ Ask your students the very same questions we just asked.
♦ Discuss risk taking with your students.
♦ Let your students share risks they have taken along with the outcomes.
♦ Make it clear that you want them to take positive risks in your classroom. (Since we're dealing with children, it is important to explain that it is not okay to take negative risks such as hitting a classmate and risking getting caught.)
♦ Ensure that your students know that making mistakes is inevitable for people who are brave enough to take risks.
♦ When a student takes a risk and fails, be supportive and encouraging so that he feels safe enough to risk again.
♦ Guide students in thinking things through when they are about to take a risk, weighing the pros and cons beforehand.
♦ Share some risks that you have taken.

Done!

It's scary trying something new when the outcome is unknown
But if you had never taken risks, you never would have grown!

DAY 104

Think About It

One of the secrets of highly successful teachers is that they know what to overlook. They see everything that goes on inside of their classrooms, but many things they pretend not to see! They always remember that children will be children, and they will ALWAYS make child-like, not adult-like decisions. On the other side of that, less effective teachers don't overlook anything. They stop for every little distraction and they end up spending the majority of their time running around putting out fires.

Ms. E. Fective was teaching a lesson. A student was tapping his pencil on his desk. Ms. E. Fective kept teaching, pretending not to notice. Since she moved around the room constantly, it did not seem strange that she just happened to pause as she got to that particular student's desk. She did not, however, make eye contact with the student. She simply paused. She was holding a class discussion and eventually she asked that student a question. He answered, she praised him, and the pencil tapping stopped.

Ms. Gotcha was teaching a lesson. A student was tapping his pencil on his desk. Ms. Gotcha walked quickly toward the student and said, "Stop it!" "What?" asked the student. "You know what!" said Ms. Gotcha. "I wasn't doing anything!" said the student. "Yes you were!" replied Ms. Gotcha. And, well, we don't need to tell you the rest of the story.

Do It

The following are some types of behavior that can often be overlooked:

♦ An occasional whisper between two students
♦ A student making odd noises for attention
♦ A student who is distracted
♦ A student mumbling under his or her breath
♦ Quiet laughter between two students

Look at the list and evaluate the types of behavior in your classroom that you do or do not overlook. Make a special effort today to overlook by hook or by crook!

Done!

Effective teachers often find that, to some behavior, it's best to remain blind.

Think About It

Some students in our classrooms lead lonely lives. Whether they're ignored at home or ignored at school or whether they lack certain social graces that would help them to establish a supportive network of friends, the fact remains that some students just don't quite fit in. From these students, we often see odd behavior—acting out in a desperate attempt for attention or shutting down and withdrawing into themselves, drowning in loneliness. Imagine if someone could throw such a student a life preserver!

Do It

Today's activity is to choose one student—one who could use some positive attention, one who just doesn't quite fit in, one who may be struggling socially, academically, or both—and *adopt* him or her. Make that student your *project* for the rest of the year. Put extra effort into that student and make sure he knows you care about him. Make sure he knows that there is someone in his life who thinks he is special and worthwhile. Smile at him every time he enters your room or every time you see him in the hallway. Ask an occasional favor of him, such as having him deliver something to the office for you.

We are not suggesting that you show outward favoritism to this student so that it is noticed and resented by other students. As we've said before, every student needs to believe he or she is your favorite. We are simply reminding you that some students need a few extra smiles from you or a more frequent pat on the back. Some students are more lacking in social skills than others. Some just don't ever quite fit in with anyone. But you can do something to change that by *adopting* such a student. You won't have difficulty finding him, because he is in every classroom.

Done!

I didn't fit in so I just shut down
Sometimes I felt I was sure to drown
But in your classroom, teacher, I was loved, not ignored
You saved me with kindness—and my confidence, you restored
And so I owe to you, teacher, a great big giant thank you
And on my list of heroes, number one is where I rank you!

DAY 105

Think About It

We are often asked, "Is it too late to try to reestablish control of students if you have lost control of them?" The answer is a resounding NO. It's never too late to start over.

None of us are perfect. In fact, there has never been a perfect teacher—ever! But one of the attributes that separates great teachers from all the rest is that they know how to quickly recover and reestablish control if they lose it. An effective teacher shared the following technique with us. We love it and we think you will too!

"My students think that I go to a teacher meeting every weekend! Whenever I feel that I need to regain some control or if I have a procedure that is no longer working, I simply say to my students, 'At the teacher meeting this weekend, they were sharing a high school procedure, and I told them my middle school students could do it. They said there was no way, but I insisted that you guys could handle this high school procedure. Would you like to try it?' They always agree, and then I just implement the new procedure. Then I tell them I can't wait until next weekend when I can brag about them at the teacher meeting!"

Do It

Try the *teacher meeting* technique with your students. If, for instance, your students are no longer following your procedure for getting quiet, then decide on a new signal you will use to get their attention and tell them you learned it at the teacher meeting! Then implement it consistently and calmly and praise them profusely when they follow it!

We know the technique works because we've shared it with thousands of teachers and have received so much positive feedback. The real beauty in the technique is that you are simply implementing something new, as opposed to appearing that you have lost control and are trying desperately to reestablish it. The students never figure it out!

Done!

Of all the students over the years to whom knowledge I've imparted
I'm yet to meet a single one who couldn't be outsmarted!

DAY 107

Think About It

Would you agree that some of your students, regardless of the age level you teach, are more responsible than others? It's a fact. And it's a tough struggle trying to teach responsibility to those who need it most. However, there is a trick to that. One of the best ways to help a student to become more responsible is by giving him more responsibility!

We've seen it tried, over and over: An adult makes the point that a child is not responsible and tells the child he needs to become more responsible. The adult is usually not happy during this conversation, and neither is the child. Where's the motivation to become more responsible? You can punish the child. True. And we're not suggesting that there is not a proper time and circumstance for punishment. We ARE suggesting, however, that continuing to point out what is negative and expecting a positive result does not usually produce a positive result. Telling a child he's bad will simply not make him good. But providing opportunities for him to be good and then praising him when he actually is good will increase the likelihood that he will be more motivated to continue to be good!

Do It

Try a simple experiment today. Take one of your most irresponsible students and give him just a little bit (don't overdo it) of responsibility. Then praise him when he acts responsibly and say, "Have you noticed that you're becoming more responsible? I'm proud of you!" Gradually, add to his experiences of being responsible, and praise him every time he acts responsibly. That's all there is to it. Now don't expect perfect responsibility overnight from your most irresponsible student. In fact, don't expect perfection from any student. Just do what all great teachers do by constantly helping your students to take small steps toward a bigger and better goal.

Done!

I had a susceptibility to portray irresponsibility
But by giving me responsibility, you increased the probability
That there was a possibility that I had capability
To now portray the ability to act with responsibility!

Think About It

One of the biggest mistakes a teacher can make is to reprimand a student in front of his peers. When you do that, you give the student an audience, and he will almost always feel a need to perform. But when you speak with a student privately, especially if it is to discuss a problem, you take away his defenses.

Any teacher can attest to the fact that a student is not nearly as *tough* when you speak to him privately, right outside of the classroom door. Another mistake teachers sometimes make is to think they are dealing with a situation privately by whispering to a student at his desk. The teacher is being discrete, and that is good. What's not good is that there is still an audience, so the student may still feel a need to perform in front of his peers even if the teacher is speaking softly to him at his desk.

Do It

Remember that reprimanding a student privately accomplishes the following:

♦ Maintains the student's dignity
♦ Removes a *stage* on which he can perform for his *audience*
♦ Lessens the likelihood that he will respond defensively
♦ Promotes the opportunity to calmly discuss the problem and its solution

Just imagine how you would want your principal to deal with you if he or she were to feel a need to reprimand you? Would you prefer for it to happen privately or in a faculty meeting? But what if you had really done something that warranted the reprimand? It doesn't matter. You'd still want for that discussion to take place in private. It's no different for the students. Always reprimand students privately.

Done!

If you deal with a problem in private, confidentially
The chances for good results improve exponentially!

Be Proactive

Think About It

Do you know what it looks like when a student is *about to misbehave*? When a student is even *thinking* about misbehaving? Of course you do! All teachers can recognize certain warning signs alerting them to the possibility that a student is feeling mischievous and possibly preparing to act on that feeling. On Day 92, we discussed ways to "nip it in the bud" when a student does not understand a concept. Today, we'll talk about "nipping it in the bud" when a student is preparing to misbehave.

One of the best ways to keep students behaving well is to be proactive. In order to be proactive, you must be constantly aware of what is going on around you in the classroom and nip those potential discipline problems in the bud. Once the misbehavior occurs, it's never too late to deal with it, but it is much more effective not to allow it to happen in the first place. Is this always possible? No. But is it often possible? Absolutely.

Do It

The next time a student is about to misbehave, try one of the following:

♦ Ask the student a question (not related to the potential misbehavior), and change the student's focus.
♦ Walk over to the student and simply stand next to him for a while.
♦ When a student is out of his desk, obviously walking over to another student to cause trouble, say something like, "Thanks, John, for going back to your desk. I appreciate that."
♦ If a student is visibly upset about something, take him aside and speak with him about what's bothering him.
♦ Get the student busy, as oftentimes boredom leads to misbehavior.

What you don't want to do is say something like, "Don't you dare." Instead, try to defuse the situation calmly and professionally. If at all possible, don't even let the student know that you knew he was about to misbehave.

Done!

Keep your eyes wide open and look for any sign
That a student's behavior is about to decline!

Think About It

On Day 22, we expressed our belief that the biggest mistake you can ever make as a teacher is to let a student know he has gotten to you personally. We've all done it at one time or another, and we can all attest to the fact that it only makes bad situations worse. And to worsen matters even further, some teachers end up engaging in power struggles with their students, arguing back and forth. Here are a few examples:

Student: I'm not going to do it!
Teacher: Oh, yes you will!

Student: Why?
Teacher: Because I said so!

Teacher: Pay attention!
Student: I *was* paying attention!
Teacher: No you weren't!

We are, of course, only giving you the beginnings of the conversations, and you can imagine where those lead.

Do It

Decide, today, how you will handle a student's attempt to engage you in a power struggle the next time it occurs. Make a commitment to remind yourself that you are the adult, that you will not engage in a power struggle with a student, that you will never "argue" with a student, and that you will remain calm and professional no matter what the student says or does. This way, only one person will walk away looking out of control, and it won't be you! Also, remember that you always have the option to say to a student, "I'll speak with you when you calm down," and then walk away. Trying to reason with someone while he is acting irrationally is always futile. Take control of the situation by being in control of yourself.

Done!

Be a sage, and don't engage
In a struggle for power with a student
Just act like an adult and let the end result
Be one where you're professional, not imprudent.

Think About It

Ah, the dreaded day when you are absent and a substitute teacher takes your place. . . . Well, it's dreaded by you and delightfully anticipated by your students. Students can experience a complete personality change when a substitute teacher enters the room. But by preparing in advance and using a little creativity, this potential problem can be averted.

Do It

The following is used, successfully, by many teachers at all grade levels.

♦ Tell your students that, because you trust them, you will turn over much of your own responsibilities to them when a substitute teacher takes your place.

♦ Assign roles to each student to play in the event that you are absent. For instance, one student will welcome the teacher. One will show the teacher where you keep your lesson plans. One will show the teacher your typical signal for getting students' attention. One will explain the daily procedures to the teacher. One will collect student work upon completion of an assignment. One will begin the applause for the teacher when the bell rings. (Don't laugh, it works!) One will give a small gift (that you will keep in a closet somewhere) to the teacher when class is over. Everyone will thank the teacher on the way out of the room.

♦ You get the point. Just create enough jobs so that each student takes on responsibility in helping the day to run as smoothly as possible.

♦ Practice this plan, several times, in anticipation of a substitute teacher. It's worth the time and effort!

When you give students responsibility, they usually rise to the occasion. This particular plan for substitute teachers has proven to work wonders at all grade levels. The students love it, and the substitute teachers are usually shocked by such a pleasant experience. Then, of course, you get the opportunity to praise your students upon your return. Just as you prepare for a fire with fire drills, do the same in anticipation of having a substitute teacher.

Done!

Don't be scared when a substitute comes. Just let the students ensure that the classroom hums
like the well-oiled machine that works when you're there. How do you do this? Prepare, prepare, prepare!

DAY 112

Think About It

"Okay, students, we have a minute until the bell rings. If you can be quiet, I won't give you anything else to do." Sound familiar? Have you ever made this mistake? What happens if you give your students even a minute with nothing to do? They will ALWAYS find something to do, and it will never be what you had in mind. We all know that students cannot handle idle time. Therefore, we have to teach from bell to bell. We cannot allow for time when students have nothing to do, hoping and praying they won't misbehave or begging some to be quiet while others finish their work. As we discussed on Day 63, effective teachers intentionally keep their students so busy that the students can't find time to misbehave!

We have learned that teachers who keep their students busy from bell to bell share a few commonalities:

♦ They plan short activities as opposed to activities that last 15, 20, or 30 minutes. This is because they know that if they assign an activity that may take 15 minutes, some will be finished in 5 minutes and others will never finish in 15 minutes. If there is an assignment or activity that requires more than a few minutes to complete, they provide frequent breaks and discussions throughout.

♦ They vary their activities to ensure student interest and engagement.

♦ They walk around monitoring while students are engaged in completing assignments.

♦ They plan for quick, smooth transitions between activities.

♦ They overplan so that they never run out of activities to keep their students engaged and learning from bell to bell.

Do It

Look at the list and determine which item, if any, you may be able to improve upon. Choose just one, and begin, today, to practice improving in that particular area. Also, begin to notice today when students tend to be off task. You should notice that off-task behavior occurs either when they are bored with an activity, when they don't understand something, or when they have nothing to do.

Done!

Give me nothing to do, and something to do I'll find
So give me something to do that will occupy my mind!

Think About It

FACT: The farther you are from a student, the more likely he or she is to misbehave. That's just human nature. Students also believe that if they are seated far away from the teacher (i.e., the back row), then the teacher won't see them misbehaving. Oftentimes, they are correct! This occurs in the classrooms of teachers who tend to "hang out" in the front of the room at most times.

Great teachers make a conscious effort to move around their classrooms constantly. You can never predict where they will be next. You never know if they are standing next to a particular student's desk just because they happen to be there or if they are standing there because the student was misbehaving or was about to misbehave. These teachers move around their rooms continually, and the students are accustomed to it. There is no advantage to sitting in the back of a great teacher's classroom! And teachers who move around the room frequently enjoy more active student engagement and better student behavior.

Do It

If someone were to ask your students, "Where does your teacher usually stand," could they answer that question? If so, you may want to begin making a conscious effort to move away from your typical hangout area. This way, when a student is misbehaving or is about to misbehave, he won't find it strange that you suddenly just happen to be standing next to him. Whether or not he knows that you noticed his behavior is really irrelevant. The point is that the behavior will almost always improve! An added bonus is that moving around the room makes you more aware of which students need your help at any given time.

Done!

Our teacher moves all over the room
And so it is not safe to assume
That sitting farther to the back
Means we can talk or we can slack
Because she's here and then she's there
Our teacher is always everywhere!

DAY 113

DAY 114

Think About It

Show us a student who is yearning for learning, and we'll show you a student who will achieve beyond measure. Show us a student who has more ability than most but does not yearn for learning, and we'll show you a struggling student and an exasperated teacher.

Therefore, it is vitally important that we help our students to yearn for learning—that we light a fire in them so that they actually hunger for the content we feed them. How do we do that? We appear that we, too, are yearning for learning and that everything we teach is the most exciting thing we have ever taught!

Do It

Is everything you teach the most exciting thing you've ever taught? No. Do the students have to THINK that everything you teach is the most exciting thing you've ever taught? Only if you want them to succeed to the best of their abilities.

Starting today, begin each lesson by telling them, excitedly, "Guess what we are going to learn today!" Then tell them, with exaggerated enthusiasm, about what they will be learning. Remember that your enthusiasm is contagious and thus becomes their enthusiasm. Enthusiastic teachers have more enthusiastic students. They have to believe that you believe before they'll ever yearn to achieve!

Done!

I'm yearning for learning
A fire in me is burning
For my teacher lights that fire in me each day
And better grades I'm earning
As the gears in my brain are churning
And I hang on every word she has to say
I'm yearning for learning
To this class I love returning
To help me succeed, my teacher finds a way!

Think About It

Why is it that some students are just plain easier to like than others? That some students are easier to believe in than others? That some students are easier to teach than others? Why can't we like each and believe in each equally? The answer is simple: We are human. But, as we reminded you on Day 34, the students cannot know that you do not like them and believe in them all equally. Next questions: Have you ever just felt like giving up on a student? You've simply tried everything you know, and you just can't reach him or get him to behave or become motivated? Again, it's human nature to become discouraged when you are experiencing a lack of success and to want to throw in the towel. But you can't do it.

All students, especially the ones who are least easy to like and least likely to behave and least likely to achieve, deserve a caring, competent teacher who refuses to give up on them. Consider the fact that the sickest patients are the ones who need doctors who refuse to give up on them. It is no different with students. But sometimes, because we are human and because we can become tired and frustrated, we all need to be reminded never to give up on any child no matter how tired or frustrated we become.

Do It

Write the names of all students on whom you may, at times, be tempted to give up. Don't leave out a single one.

_____

_____

_____

_____

_____

Then do one thing for each—don't give up! By that we mean keep reminding yourself why you chose teaching, talk to others to get ideas if you feel you have tried everything you know, and, most importantly, make it clear to all of these students that you care about them, that you believe in them, and that you will not give up on them.

Done!

Please do not give up on me. Never give up on me—NEVER!
'Cause if you don't, I promise I won't ever forget you, EVER!

DAY 116

Think About It

Who is the most positive person on the faculty at your school? Get that person's face in your mind. Think about what it is that makes you regard that person as the most positive person on the faculty. And now for the important question: Is it you? If your coworkers were asked to name the most positive person on the faculty, would they name you? If so, why? If not, why not?

On Day 86, we discussed the importance of your reputation with your students. Today, we are focusing on your reputation with the faculty. Though it should never be your goal to get everyone on the faculty to like you and/or agree with you, it is important to be viewed as a positive, professional person.

Do It

Even if you didn't think of yourself when you were thinking of the most positive person on the faculty, the good news is that you can absolutely become that person today! Here are the types of behavior you want to display in order to become viewed, by everyone on the faculty, as the most positive teacher on the faculty:

♦ Displays a cheerful demeanor
♦ Speaks well of students
♦ Speaks well of others
♦ Does not participate in gossip-sharing sessions
♦ Always acts professionally, even in times of disagreement
♦ Is viewed as an advocate for students
♦ Is willing to lend support to coworkers
♦ Participates in schoolwide activities

Done!

Let's face it: Being positive makes the negative people around you uncomfortable. This is a good thing! So though you very likely will not be best buddies with negative teachers, you'll still be viewed by them as positive and professional, much to their dismay. Again, this is a good thing.

When the negative teachers are intimidated by your glee
You know you're behaving professionally!

Think About It

If I do something nice for you
And you do something nice for another
And the third person pays it forward, too
For a friend or a stranger or brother
Then I am directly responsible
For igniting a chain reaction
Of good deeds spreading to the ends of the earth
And it started with one interaction.

Do It

Today's activity is to read the preceding poem to your students and have a brief discussion with them about what can happen when one person does one good deed for another, expecting nothing in return.

Tell your students that their homework today is as follows:

1. Do one good deed for someone in this class.
2. If someone in this class does something nice for you, pay it forward by doing a good deed for someone else in this class.
3. The only rule is that it has to stay within the class for now. In other words, if someone in the class does something nice for you, you have to pay it forward to someone else in this class.

Do you see where this is leading? You're starting a chain reaction in your classroom among your students. By making the rule that it has to stay within the class, you are helping students to be nicer to each other!

On an added note, we suggest that you participate in this also. You will act as a safety valve so that if one student does not have someone doing something nice for him, you can step in and be the person to do something nice for him. This way, no one is left out.

Done!

Tell the students that tomorrow, you will ask each to share what he or she did to pay it forward to someone.

DAY 117

Pay It Forward, Part 2

Today's activity has three parts:

1. Allow each student to tell you something he or she did to "pay it forward" to another student in the class. If you don't have time to get to everyone, you can take a few minutes to finish tomorrow. Here, you may want to write about who did what for whom:

    _____
    _____
    _____
    _____
    _____
    _____
    _____
    _____
    _____

2. Ask each student to write one sentence about what he or she did to pay it forward after someone in the class did something nice for him or her. Then say, "If no one in the class did something to pay it forward to you yet, that's okay. Just write your name and leave your paper blank." This, of course, will be your cue to do something nice for that student.

    _____
    _____
    _____
    _____
    _____
    _____
    _____
    _____
    _____

3. Tell your students that tonight's homework will be to go home and pay it forward to someone who is NOT in the class. You will ask them to share these tomorrow.

Think About It

For the last two days, you have taken a few minutes a day to not only start your own chain reaction of good deeds spreading to others, but you've enabled students to start their own such chain reactions. The goal, of course, is to introduce them to the idea of doing good deeds for others, expecting nothing in return. As a teacher, you perform good deeds each day. You truly will never know how far your influence will reach!

Do It

Either discuss or have students write what they did to pay it forward to someone who is not in the class. It's very beneficial to have them share these aloud. But if a student does not, for whatever reason, want to share his or her good deed, say, "That's okay. You have the option to write it and just turn it in to me."

Here, you may want to jot notes to yourself regarding your students' reactions to this assignment:

_____

_____

_____

_____

_____

_____

_____

_____

_____

_____

_____

_____

_____

Done!

You've now been directly responsible
For igniting a chain reaction
Of good deeds that may spread to the ends of the earth
And it started with one interaction.

DAY 119

20-Day Reality Check

Following is a simple survey for you to complete based on all topics we have discussed since the previous 20-Day Reality Check. Your assignment today is simply to complete the survey. For each statement, write "Yes" or "No" in the right-hand column.

Survey

1	I have used the "avoid a wreck checklist" from Day 102.	
2	I'm helping students become comfortable with positive risk taking.	
3	I make an effort to overlook minor misbehavior whenever possible.	
4	I have "adopted" a troubled student.	
5	I have tried the "teacher meeting" technique (or something similar) from Day 106.	
6	I am helping to make irresponsible students more responsible by slowly giving them more responsibility.	
7	I deal with student behavior issues privately.	
8	I spot warning signs telling me that students are about to misbehave, and I use proactive techniques to stop the misbehavior before it occurs.	
9	I do not engage in power struggles with students.	
10	I have implemented and practiced with my students some type of plan for substitute teachers.	
11	I teach from bell to bell.	
12	I make a conscious effort to move around the room as I teach.	
13	I use my own enthusiasm to spark enthusiasm in my students.	
14	I am working at being the most positive teacher on the faculty.	
15	I am encouraging my students to "pay it forward."	

What I Learned/What I'll Do Differently

Based on yesterday's survey results, take a few minutes to list what you have learned, what you may have already known but needed to be reminded of, what you've noticed about your students, what you will attempt to do differently in your teaching from this point forward.

DAY 121

Think About It

I stood at a fork in the road
And I didn't know which way to go
But since I had no destination in mind
If I got there, I'd never know . . .

Do It

On Day 88, we talked about the fact that so few people have clear, written goals, but the few who do have written goals accomplish far more than all of the others combined! You discussed the importance of goal-setting with your students and had them write goals for themselves.

And now for a very important question: Do YOU have written goals for yourself? What kind of teacher do you want to become? How much do you want to accomplish with your students by the end of the year? Do you have plans to learn new teaching techniques this year? Do you want to earn a higher degree or further your certification? Do you aspire to become a leader of other teachers?

Your activity today is to come up with at least one goal you have for yourself as a professional educator. Just the simple act of writing this goal (or goals) puts you way ahead of most. Be realistic, but aim high.

_____

_____

_____

_____

_____

_____

_____

_____

_____

_____

Done!

Simply writing a goal is a VERY important step. But now you must set that written plan into action. Begin taking small steps each day toward achieving your goals.

Think About It

As the old saying goes, "Blessed are the flexible, for they shall not be bent out of shape." This may be truer of teachers than of people in any other profession. Effective teachers are masters at being flexible. They have to be! If you're the kind of person who has to have all your ducks in a row all the time and who gets rattled when one of your ducks swims away, then you cannot be a teacher. If you need to know what is going to happen, routinely, every second of your day and you become disgruntled when even one of your planned activities does not go as planned, then you cannot be a teacher. If you need predictability in your life, then you cannot be a teacher. Teaching is unpredictable. Students are unpredictable. Learning is unpredictable. You simply have to be flexible in order to teach effectively.

Do It

Your activity for today is to add to our list of the many unpredictabilities of teaching:

♦ Fire drills, tornado drills, lock-down drills
♦ Meetings that crop up out of nowhere
♦ Unexpected announcements from the front office
♦ Knocks at your door while you are teaching
♦ Well-planned lessons not going as planned
♦ Students' home lives affecting their learning and/or behavior

♦ _____
♦ _____
♦ _____
♦ _____
♦ _____

Now pat yourself on the back for being able to juggle so much every day. Remind yourself how important it is to be flexible on a daily basis when dealing with students. And remind yourself that though it is vitally important to plan every minute of your teaching every day, your day will never go completely as planned.

Done!

No way around it; no way to pretend
You're sure to break if you cannot bend.

DAY 124

Think About It

We often remind teachers that one of the best ways to squelch negative behavior is simply to defuse it. After hearing us speak of this, a teacher shared the following with us:

> I wasn't sure if your idea about defusing negative behavior would work, but I was willing to give it a try. Class had just begun and a student raised her hand and complained that the student behind her was singing. I went to the singing student and said, in a very enthusiastic way, "Oh, I love to sing, too! What song were you singing?" He told me the name of the song and I said, "I love that song, and I bet you sing it well. It's not appropriate to sing it now, but I've always wanted to learn that song. Would you mind coming in during lunch period and teaching it to me? We could perform a duet! See you at lunch!" Of course, he did not show up to teach it to me, but he never sang in class again! Mission accomplished!

This teacher's principal later spoke with us and said, "She used to have lots of discipline problems because she would argue with her students. Now that she has learned how to defuse negative behavior, her discipline problems are almost nonexistent. Once the power struggles stopped, the students stopped trying to push her buttons. She's a happier person and the students are so much better behaved now."

Do It

If you remove the fuse from a firecracker, you cannot ignite it. Period. If you leave the fuse intact and add fire to it, BAM! Fill in the blanks here with ideas for defusing these potentially explosive situations:

♦ A student walks into class in a very bad mood. Instead of telling him that he had better check his bad attitude at the door, I will try

_____

♦ A student is visibly frustrated while taking his test. He throws his paper on the floor and puts his head down. Instead of telling him to pick it up and get busy, I will try

_____

♦ A chronic "tattler" is tattling on another student, yet again. Instead of telling him to stop worrying about what everyone else is doing, I will try

_____

Done!

Once the fuse is removed, the behavior is improved.

Gossip Never Charms—It Harms!

Think About It

Let's begin with a very important fact: Gossip serves one purpose—it harms! None of us entered this profession to harm anyone, yet some teachers engage in what they consider to be "harmless gossip." No such thing! And please remember that if someone will gossip WITH you, they will also gossip ABOUT you. Gossiping also harms YOU, because it makes you appear unprofessional and petty. So just commit to NOT speaking ill of others, period!

But isn't it true that sometimes you just happen to be in the wrong place at the wrong time? You're just minding your own business and the gossip begins in your presence. You surely did not start it, and you certainly don't want to be a part of it, but what can you do?

Do It

We'll share with you two of our favorite techniques for defusing a negative coworker who wants to spread gossip and/or warn you about students, parents, administration, or others.

1. If a teacher attempts to warn you about one or more of your students, simply say, "I'm so glad to have that student (or those students) in my classroom because students like these need me more than anyone. I can tell you're sharing this information out of concern, so I promise to treat him with extra special attention, and I'll keep you posted on his progress. Thanks."
2. If a teacher approaches you and tries to speak ill of someone, simply say, "I can't speak with you right now because I'm on my way to the bathroom. I'll speak with you later. See ya!" This technique works wonders because gossip is *hot* and so they quickly share it with someone else and forget about sharing it with you!

Done!

If you can't say something good about another, don't speak
About students or parents, don't let gossip leak
Walk away from a coworker wanting to say
A negative word about another today.

Think About It

"Why do we have to know this?" Students ask this question on a regular basis. And whenever the question is asked, it should be a red flag to the teacher that he or she has not made the connection between the skill being taught and the student's actual life experiences and reality.

If you were a student, to which lesson would you relate?

1. A lesson about pronouns where you learn that a pronoun takes the place of a noun and then you practice finding pronouns in sentences and underlining them.
2. A lesson where you are asked to tell something about yourself without using any of the words on the board (which are all pronouns).

Here's another example. To which do you think students would more favorably respond?

1. A worksheet with problems where students have to determine the area of given rectangles.
2. Getting into a group and determining the area of a rectangular bulletin board and then using that information to tell the teacher how much paper they will need to cover the board that they will then decorate?

We won't insult you by giving you the answers. The bottom line is that students want to learn when they see that what they are learning is relevant!

Do It

Look at the concepts you are teaching today and ask yourself, How am I ensuring that the students know how this concept relates to their lives? Oh, and by the way, you want to relate the concept to their lives today as opposed to their futures. To tell a student, "You need to know this because it will help you to get a job one day" is basically pointless. So relate what you teach to their real lives TODAY.

Done!

Making it real has tremendous appeal. If your students understand why they learn what they learn, motivation will increase and better grades they'll earn.

Your Study Buddy

Think About It

As teachers, we often feel "isolated" from one another. We spend our days in our classrooms with our students and often don't have much time to interact with our colleagues. But we often get wonderful ideas or answers to our questions from our colleagues, and we can all benefit from one another's support. And let's face it: Sometimes we just need to communicate with other adults!

It's often easier to accomplish a task if you have a "buddy" to help you. It's often easier to deal with a difficult situation if you have a "buddy" to lend a listening ear. And it's always more motivating to accomplish a task if you have someone in your corner cheering you on!

Do It

Get yourself a "Study Buddy." Form an agreement with a teacher who teaches near you. You may even want to turn it into a competition. Here are some ideas for your agreement or competition:

♦ See which of you can go the longest without losing your cool or getting your buttons visibly pushed. Have some type of prize. Whoever wins the competition wins the prize!
♦ Agree that you will each put extra effort into helping a troubled student, and then share your successes with one another.
♦ Share lesson ideas or ideas for improving achievement or behavior.
♦ See who can come up with the most creative way to get students to accomplish a given task, or turn in homework, or read the most books, etc.
♦ Have your two classes occasionally compete with one another for things like attendance, turning in homework, good behavior, and such.

Selecting a buddy is like choosing a tennis partner. Practicing with someone better than you can help boost your game.

Done!

I have a study buddy—
The teacher across the hall
We climb the teaching ladder each day
But sometimes we trip and fall
So we're "spotting" one another now
And lending a helping hand
If one of us falls, we don't hit the ground
For in the other's arms we land.

Don't Be a Deflator of Your Administrator

Think About It

Do you like your principal and other administrators? Do you not like your principal and other administrators? Either way, there's good news: You don't spend much time with your administrators, right? Most teachers will agree that they spend about 90 percent of each school day with their students. And most will also agree that they spend less than one percent of each school day with their administrators. Though we definitely agree that an effective administrator is very important in any school, great teachers continue to remind us that great teachers are still great teachers even in schools with less-than-effective administrators.

So why is it that some teachers seem to spend a lot of their time complaining about someone with whom they spend less than one percent of their day? Doesn't it make more sense to put 100 percent of your efforts into the people with whom you spend more than 90 percent of each school day?

Do It

It will never happen that you agree with everything your administrator does or does not do. So, if you feel strongly about an issue with which you disagree, discuss it privately and professionally with your administrator. But if the issue is one over which you have no control, let it go. Focus on what you can control, not on what you can't. Most importantly, do your utmost to work in cooperation with and support of your administration. Do this for the betterment of the school and ultimately the students. Don't get caught up in petty issues that lead to breakdowns in communication and cooperation.

Done!

Even if you sometimes view your administrator as a dictator
The time you spend complaining about your administrator should not be greater
Than the amount of time you spend in the presence of said administrator
So try to be a cooperator as opposed to another problem creator.

Attention, Again, All Parents!

On Day 42, you sent a letter to all of your students' parents, sharing some exciting and positive things that were happening in your classroom. As we stated then, ALL parents like to hear good news from their children's teachers. So today's activity will simply be to send another letter, just like you did on Day 42, providing them with an update on what their children are accomplishing in your classroom.

Remember, just one note, not one to every parent, saying something like the following:

At the secondary level, you can decide if one letter is appropriate for all classes or if each class needs different details. You could write one a day for a week and cover five classes in a short period of time.

Remember Your Favorite Teacher

Think About It

All students have favorite teachers. Not surprisingly, students' reasons for considering these teachers favorites are usually quite similar. Think back to your own days in school. Think about your favorite teacher—the one who, for many reasons, stood above all the rest. Get that person's name or face in your mind. Think about what it was that made you consider that particular teacher your favorite. Doesn't it make you want to smile just thinking about that teacher?

Do It

Now that you have thought about your favorite teacher, take a minute to fill in the blanks:

♦ My favorite teacher made me feel _____

♦ My favorite teacher never made me feel _____

♦ My favorite teacher's demeanor was _____

♦ My favorite teacher treated me _____

♦ My favorite teacher always _____

♦ What I remember most about my favorite teacher is _____

_____

♦ If I had to describe my favorite teacher in one word, it would be

_____

If we were to substitute this list with your name in the place of "my favorite teacher," and ask your students to fill in the blanks, would they provide similar answers to those you have given?

Done!

We end this segment with one suggestion: Treat your students like your favorite teacher treated you and others.

Remember Your Least Favorite Teacher

Think About It

All students have least favorite teachers. Not surprisingly, students' reasons for considering these teachers least favorites are usually quite similar. Think back to your own days in school. Think about your least favorite teacher. Get that person's name or face in your mind. Think about what it was that made you consider that particular teacher to be your least favorite. Isn't it a little painful just thinking about that teacher?

Do It

Now that you have thought about your least favorite teacher, take a minute to fill in the blanks:

- My least favorite teacher made me feel _____
- My least favorite teacher never made me feel _____
- My least favorite teacher's demeanor was _____
- My least favorite teacher treated me _____
- My least favorite teacher always _____
- What I remember most about my least favorite teacher is _____
  _____
- If I had to describe my least favorite teacher in one word, it would be
  _____

Done!

We end this segment with one suggestion: Do not ever treat your students like your least favorite teacher treated you or others.

DAY 132

Think About It

Homework . . . Just the word itself can elevate the blood pressures of most teachers. Students complain about it, parents complain about it, and teachers complain about the fact that some students do not do it. When a student doesn't do it, it often turns into a power struggle with the teacher who assigned it.

As the saying goes, "Everything in moderation." Students spend long hours at school each day, so it is understandable that they don't relish the thought of doing more schoolwork when they get home. We are not against homework. We're simply against too much of it. When you do assign it, make it meaningful and doable. But even when homework is meaningful and doable, most teachers still struggle with at least one or two students who fail, on a consistent basis, to do it. And though there is no *magic strategy* for getting all students to do their homework, we will share a technique with you that will help to improve the odds that they might just do it this time.

Do It

The goal today is to set your students up for success. Give them a short, meaningful homework assignment. Make it simple, because you're trying to get them all to turn in their homework tomorrow. For instance, if you're learning about nouns, the assignment might be as follows: *Go home tonight and open a junk drawer. Everyone has a junk drawer! List ten nouns you find in your junk drawer.*

You can relate the *idea* behind this to your particular subject area. The point is that this type of assignment is much more likely to be completed than one involving a worksheet with ten sentences where they have to underline the nouns in each sentence. Tell them you have a surprise for anyone who turns in their homework assignment tomorrow. The surprise can be that anyone who does the assignment is exempt from the next assignment or it can be a sticker or anything else you deem appropriate. Remember that even high school students love receiving stickers from a teacher they hold in high regard.

Done!

Though we are not suggesting that you reward students every time they do homework, understand that what we are doing today is trying to set students up for success. Today's assignment is doable, it's not overwhelming, it may even be fun, and there's a reward attached. There. Chances of success have just improved.

Think About It

Teachers have battled students over homework since the invention of homework. A typical scenario is that a teacher assigns homework and then collects it. A student who does not do it either gets a zero or is now required to double the amount. But if he didn't do it once, he probably won't do it twice . . . A power struggle ensues, and the teacher usually doesn't win.

Yesterday, you gave a simple homework assignment with a perk attached. You told students that you would have a surprise today for anyone who completed the assignment. As a reminder, the real point in this particular assignment was to set each student up for a successful experience with homework, especially those who don't typically experience much success doing that. You see, if you can get a student who doesn't typically do homework to actually do his homework, you can praise him for it, thereby increasing the likelihood that he may do it again in the future. That's the goal. But what if he still doesn't turn it in? Read on.

Do It

Collect yesterday's homework assignment. Go over it quickly, and be sure to praise all students who completed their assignments. Give each his reward. It is likely that most students completed the assignment, if for no other reason than to receive the prize. Thank them, and tell them you appreciate their sense of responsibility. Tell them you notice that they are becoming more and more responsible regarding homework. That's it.

If a student has not turned in the assignment, employ another little trick. Say to the student, "I need for you to deliver something to the office for me tomorrow." (Students love to run errands.) "But I'll probably forget tomorrow, so just put a note on top of your homework tomorrow, the assignment that you forgot to turn in today. When you turn it in, I'll see the reminder and then I'll send you on the errand. Thanks." Students are never too old for this approach.

Done!

Tomorrow, chances are good that he will turn in the homework, providing you with the opportunity to praise him. Again, we are not recommending that you always reward students for turning in homework. These last two days have simply been an attempt to provide them all with a successful homework experience.

DAY 134

Think About It

Your least prudent student is the one who needs you most
Working on unnerving you often keeps him most engrossed
But please remember, teacher, that you are the adult
The one who can take a negative situation and get a positive result!

He or she is in every classroom—our least prudent student. He's the one who talks the loudest, who aggravates others the most, who aggravates you the most, who seems to derive pleasure from the misery of others, and who makes you question your sanity. You have an advantage over him, of course, in that you are the trained professional! But sometimes even trained professionals become overwhelmed and forget that having a plan and implementing it methodically can produce positive results. Over the next five days, we'll help you to implement a simple plan for helping your least prudent student to become more prudent.

Before we go further, ask yourself, "Does this student know he is upsetting me with his behavior?" If yes, then one of the most effective ways to help him to become more prudent is to stop letting him know that. Simply decide that no matter what he does, you will not allow him to know he is aggravating you. This will help to make the next few days even more successful!

Do It

Today's activity is to find a way to compliment your least prudent student. Make sure it is a sincere compliment about something he does well or something you like about him. Regardless of his response, don't react. Just pay him the compliment and quickly move on.

Done!

Write a sentence or two describing his reaction today when you complimented him.

_____

_____

_____

_____

_____

Your Least Prudent Student, Part 2

Today, we would like for you to set up your least prudent student for success in some kind of way. If he struggles academically, then give him some type of assignment that is doable for him, and then immediately praise him for a job well done. If he struggles with behavior, then wait until he is not misbehaving and praise him for it. The key, today, is to create a way to praise him for a job well done. Use phrases such as:

♦ I'm proud of you for _____

♦ Great job doing _____

♦ I appreciate the way you _____

♦ I notice a real improvement in your work.

♦ Thanks for trying so hard.

Tell what you did to set him up for success:

_____

_____

_____

_____

_____

_____

_____

_____

Tell how the student reacted to the praise you provided when he succeeded:

_____

_____

_____

_____

_____

_____

_____

We have yet to meet a student who doesn't like to run an errand. Also, when you send a student on an errand, it gives him the message that he is important and that you care about him. These are definitely the kinds of messages you want your least prudent student to get from you. However, use your judgment. If your least prudent student is one who would very likely roam the halls causing trouble if you sent him out on his own, then don't send him down the hall. Instead, simply send him across the hall to deliver something to the neighboring classroom. This way, you can keep a watchful eye on him.

Simply decide on an errand you would like to send this student on, and send him along. When he returns, say, "Thanks so much for doing that for me. I appreciate it."

Tell about the errand:

_____

_____

_____

_____

_____

_____

_____

_____

Tell how the student reacted to you both when you sent him on the errand and when you thanked him upon his return:

_____

_____

_____

_____

_____

_____

_____

_____

DAY 136

Your Least Prudent Student, Part 4

Even to the least prudent of students, it feels good to have someone notice something nice about him. That student won't always respond by saying, "Thanks for noticing something nice about me." In fact, sometimes the reaction is quite the opposite. You may have noticed, over the last few days, that the student seems almost a little suspicious of the fact that you are giving him more positive attention than you may typically give to him. That's okay. Don't worry about his outward reactions. Just know that on the inside he is, in his own way, appreciating the attention, whether he ever lets you know that or not.

Today, notice something nice about your least prudent student and comment on it. Maybe you noticed his new haircut; maybe you like his new shirt; maybe you noticed how attentive he was during an activity; maybe you noticed that he did something nice for another. It really doesn't matter what it is that you notice as long as you notice it and comment on it.

Tell what you did to let him know you noticed something nice about him:

_____

_____

_____

_____

_____

_____

_____

_____

Tell how the student reacted to you when you noticed something nice about him:

_____

_____

_____

_____

_____

_____

_____

Your Least Prudent Student, Part 5

Over the past few days, you have taken a special interest in your least prudent student. You have complimented him for jobs well done, you have trusted him enough send him on an errand, you have noticed something nice about him, and so on. These experiences should have provided you with *something* to tell his parents in a note home.

Write a brief note to his parents today saying something like, "I'm really proud of Trevor because he has really improved in _____ ." Make sure he sees the note. Don't put it into a sealed envelope when you give it to him.

Tell what you wrote in the note:

_____
_____
_____
_____
_____
_____

Tell how the student reacted when you handed him the note:

_____
_____
_____
_____
_____
_____

Tell what you have noticed about his behavior in general now that you have been paying him so much positive attention over the last five days:

_____
_____
_____
_____
_____
_____

Think About It

Why did you become a teacher? What makes you continue to choose this profession? Why, despite the lack of pay and the seemingly endless paperwork, do you find pride in calling yourself a teacher? When did you first know that you would be a teacher?

Though specific reasons for becoming teachers differ, there are always similarities regarding why teachers choose to be teachers. Those similarities typically include:

♦ I love working with young people.
♦ I want to make a difference in someone's life.
♦ I enjoy helping others.
♦ I have a special gift for helping others to understand things with which they are struggling.
♦ I have a knack for inspiring others.
♦ I was influenced by some of my own teachers, and I wanted to do for others what my most influential teachers did for me.

Do you know that most students have no idea why their teachers have chosen to teach them? Why do you think that is? We believe it is because many teachers have never thought about how important it is for their students to know that their teachers love teaching, choose teaching, and genuinely want to help all students succeed. When students know this about their teachers, they are much more likely to learn, grow, take risks, feel safe, and behave well.

Do It

Take a minute or two today to tell your students why you chose to be a teacher, why you continue to choose teaching, and how lucky you feel to be teaching them. Let them know that you see teaching as a calling and a privilege. Let them know how important their success is to you. Students of all ages love stories, so tell them yours!

Done!

Convince me that you love what you do, and I'm much more likely to learn from you!

Following is a simple survey for you to complete based on all topics we have discussed since the previous 20-Day Reality Check. Your assignment today is simply to complete the survey. For each statement, write "Yes" or "No" in the right-hand column.

Survey

1	I have written goals for my professional growth.	
2	I know that teaching can be overwhelming and unpredictable, so I do my best to remain flexible.	
3	I use techniques to defuse negative behavior in students.	
4	I am careful not to engage in gossiping.	
5	I ensure that my lessons relate to the real lives of my students.	
6	I have tried the "Study Buddy" technique from Day 127.	
7	I am careful not to be a deflator of my administrator.	
8	I let parents know of the good things that are happening in class.	
9	I try to treat my students like my favorite teachers treated their students.	
10	I am careful never to treat my students like my least favorite teachers treated their students.	
11	I am careful not to overload students with homework.	
12	I have attempted the homework perk suggestions from Days 132 and 133.	
13	I have put extra effort into helping my least prudent student.	
14	I have shared the story of why I became a teacher with my students.	

What I Learned/What I'll Do Differently

Based on yesterday's survey results, take a few minutes to list what you have learned, what you may have already known but needed to be reminded of, what you've noticed about your students, what you will attempt to do differently in your teaching from this point forward.

_____

_____

_____

_____

_____

_____

_____

_____

_____

_____

_____

_____

_____

_____

_____

_____

_____

_____

_____

_____

_____

_____

_____

_____

_____

DAY 141

DAY 142

Think About It

Students like to play games. There's research to show that, but we, as teachers, don't even need that research to tell us what we already know. Games are engaging and motivating and fun for students. They're fun for adults, too! Great teachers often incorporate the use of games into their teaching. One of the best and easiest ways to incorporate games in the classroom is for the purpose of review. Here's one of our favorite games to use for a test review:

> Get a trash-can basketball game or one of those over-the-door indoor basketball hoops. Tell the students about the game the day before you actually play it. Since this will be a review game, you'll want to give them notice ahead of time so that they can study whatever content or skills you'll be testing. And now for the game: Ask a student a question or have him demonstrate a skill that will be on the test. If he answers correctly, he gets a point plus a shot. If he makes the shot, he gets another point. If a student answers a question incorrectly or misses his shot, he simply waits for his next turn. We like dividing the class into two teams and having the teams compete against one another. This way, students are more likely to remain engaged even when it is not their turn, and they are more apt to cheer for one another.

Do It

We provided you with one example of a game that is used successfully by teachers at all grade levels. We encourage you to play some type of game today with your students. Whatever the game, just make sure that it relates to what you are teaching and that it affords everyone an opportunity to succeed. Students love it when their teacher participates in the game, so go ahead and play along.

Done!

Break the monotony of what's routine and same
By engaging your students in a learning game!

The Confection Connection

Think About It

My teacher gave me something sweet—
A delicious, delightful confection
She gave me this sweet treat to eat
To show her appreciation and affection
When receiving this delicious surprise
I did not have any objection
And now I think my teacher
Is one step closer to perfection!

Do It

Teachers love it when they attend a meeting and refreshments are served. We often laugh at the fact that passengers on an airplane anxiously await a tiny bag of peanuts! Restaurants often provide a dish of candy for patrons as they exit the restaurant. Even if they're full to bursting, most people will put their hands into that candy dish. People enjoy receiving anything viewed as a treat. Do you remember, as a child, receiving a lollipop at the doctor's office after that painful injection? It was "almost" worth the pain!

We encourage you to occasionally provide treats for your students. Okay, so you can't afford to feed them every day, and we're not suggesting that you do that. We're simply encouraging you to bring small treats, on occasion, simply because.

Many teachers use edible treats as rewards for some type of accomplishment, and we have no objection to that. But every now and then, give them all a treat just to show them you think they're special.

Done!

What does providing your students with treats have to do with effective teaching and learning? Anything that, in any way, helps to endear your students TO you will increase their willingness to learn FROM you! Never forget that you have to reach your students before you can teach your students.

DAY 143

The Word Is Out

Think About It

Imagine having someone come up to you and say something like the following:

♦ Wow! Your boss was really singing your praises today. He says you're a wonderful teacher and he's lucky to have you on the faculty.
♦ I heard you did a great job spearheading the committee. Several people were talking about the wonderful job you did.
♦ I overheard a group of students saying you are their favorite teacher.
♦ I attended a parent meeting, and a group of parents said they will do whatever it takes to make sure their children have you as their teacher next year.

Wouldn't that feel great? Don't we all like to hear that others notice and appreciate our efforts? Knowing that people thought of you this way would make you want to be even better than you already are, right?

Do It

On Day 69, we talked about the fact that nothing does a better job of getting students on your side than to brag about them to others. You expressed your pride in your students by telling them you brag about them to your friends, family, and coworkers. Today, you will prove that.

Have one of your coworkers stop by your room and say to your students, "I just wanted you all to know that your teacher was singing your praises. She says you are some of the best students she has ever taught. She brags about you all the time." That's it. It takes about 20 seconds. But those few seconds mean a lot to your students. You can have an administrator do this or a coworker or any other adult in the school. And if you teach several classes a day, do it for every class.

Done!

To learn that someone appreciates you is really a thrilling sensation
It is one of the nicest feelings in the world to receive someone's commendation
So show your students you appreciate them, for they need that affirmation
Between praise and good behavior, there is a definite correlation!

Assess Your Stress

Think About It

The fact that *stressed* spelled backwards is *desserts* is not a good thing! As teachers, we all experience stress. But how we react to that stress is important—to our physical well-being, to our emotional well-being, and to the well-being of our students.

Do It

Assess your own stress. Do you find yourself experiencing any of the following?

- Procrastinating with paperwork
- Raising your voice at students when you get frustrated
- Reacting out of frustration and then regretting your actions
- Getting upset about things in the school over which you have no control
- Feeling overwhelmed with too much to do and not enough time to do it
- Getting into power struggles with one or more students on a fairly regular basis
- Having problems getting along with a coworker
- Having problems enlisting support of parents

These are typical stress producers for many teachers, so you are not alone if you spotted yourself. Here are a few things you can do to help to de-stress:

- Stay on top of your work load by managing your time wisely.
- Remind yourself why you chose to become a teacher. Always keep that at the forefront of any decision you make.
- Do not allow yourself to engage in power struggles with students. You always have the option to say, "I'll speak with you later about this." This gives you the opportunity to calm down, to allow the student to calm down, and to think about how you will deal with the situation.
- If there is a situation over which you have no control, let it go.
- Smile often and breathe deeply.
- Be professional with students and coworkers, no matter what.
- Never let the students know they are getting to you.

Done!

Don't beat yourself up for occasionally feeling overwhelmed. You're a hardworking professional, and stress is inevitable. Just try to remember that you are making a difference. And give yourself a break on occasion. Treat yourself to a fun night out! You've earned it.

Hocus Pocus, Focus!

Think About It

A speaker stood in front of a very large audience and said, "I'm going to give you 30 seconds to look around the room and remember everything you can that is any shade of brown. You have 30 seconds to look around and remember anything that is any shade of brown. Go!" Hundreds of people began looking all around the room for anything that was brown. The speaker counted down, saying, "Ten, nine, eight . . . Okay, close your eyes." The speaker then said, "Now remember anything you can that is any shade of white." You could see the startled faces on the audience, as no one could seem to remember anything that was white. The people who were wearing white could not even seem to remember that they were wearing white! Then the speaker said, "Now open your eyes and look around the room." To the amazement of the audience, there was white everywhere. The walls were white, the ceiling was white, the large screen on the stage was white, and there was white all over the room. There was actually much more white in the room than there was brown.

"As you can see," said the speaker, "there is much more white in the room than there is brown, but most of you could not think of a single thing that was white when your eyes were closed. Why do you think that happened?" It happened, of course, because everyone was focusing on brown. "And so," he said, "life is what you focus on. At any given time, there are positives and negatives all around you. You get to choose your focus. Focus on white!"

Do It

Your simple activity for today is to try this experiment with your students. Make the same points to your students that the speaker made to his audience. And, remember to remind yourself to focus on the positives in your life and in your classroom.

Done!

Life is what you focus upon more so than it is what occurs
The more you focus on what's positive in life, the more the negative blurs
A positive outlook, from one to another, is contagious and always transfers
And people who focus on positive things are the people everyone prefers!

How Would Your Students Describe You?

If someone were to ask your students to describe you based on the following choices, how would your students respond?

For each number, circle the choice that best describes your teacher:

1.	Nice	Mean	In between
2.	Happy	Unhappy	In between
3.	Energetic	Unenergetic	In between
4.	Loves teaching	Doesn't love teaching	I don't know
5.	Professional	Unprofessional	In between
6.	Good at teaching	Not good at teaching	In between
7.	Positive	Negative	In between
8.	Calm	Nervous	In between
9.	Organized	Disorganized	In between
10.	Makes learning fun	Doesn't make learning fun	In between
11.	Respectful	Disrespectful	In between
12.	Believes in me	Doesn't believe in me	I don't know

You don't need an answer key to know that all the first choices are reserved for only the best teachers. If you look at the list and fear that your students might not select the first choices of each when thinking of you, then work hard at convincing them otherwise. Be your best and give your students your all. And if you're REALLY brave, let your students answer the questions. Our students are our very best critics!

I'm Proud of Your Child

Think About It

Parents love to hear that someone is proud of their child, no matter how old their child is. When someone is proud of their child, they see it as a compliment to their parenting. Surely they must be doing something right if someone is proud of their child! And children love to have adults express pride in them. When you send a note home saying you're proud of a child, the child now has at least two people who are proud of him—the teacher and at least one parent.

Do It

```
Dear Mrs./Mr. _____ :
                          (parent's name)


I just wanted to say that I'm proud of _____
                                            (child's name)
for _____

_____

_____ .

I knew you would be proud too.

Sincerely:

_____
```

Try sending a few of these notes home today. These notes almost always make it to parents. And they are worth their weight in gold! Keep a few in your desk drawer and use them often.

Done!

You sent me a note—just to say
That you're proud of something my child did today
And now I, too, am swelling with pride
That I'm a good parent is what you also implied!

Think About It

There's no such thing as too much good. There will never be too many good people or too many good deeds or too many good teachers or too many good students. Children, in particular, need more good in their lives. And they need more adults recognizing the good qualities in them.

Do It

Here is your simple activity for today:

Take a large sheet of paper (for each of your classes) and write the name of each of your students in a particular class on that sheet. Next to each student's name, put two blanks. Fill in the first blank with a word or phrase describing one good quality about each student. Leave the second blank empty. For example:

1. Travis: polite   _____

2. Lauren: hard-working   _____

3. Madison: creative   _____

At the end of the day, put that piece of paper on the wall of your classroom. Make sure it is large enough for everyone to read. A piece of bulletin-board paper works great. Do this after the students leave, because you don't want them to see this until tomorrow.

Done!

Tell your students to go home tonight and think of one good quality they possess. We'll tell you what to do with that information tomorrow.

Good, Understood, Part 2

Yesterday, you posted a large sheet of paper with every student's name and a positive word or phrase describing each student next to his name. Today, write a few examples of behavior you noticed as the students walked into the room and spotted this display before you said anything to them about it.

_____

_____

_____

_____

_____

_____

_____

_____

_____

_____

_____

You most likely saw surprise and positive expressions. You most likely received questions about it. A few students may have begun to make jokes about it. That is because many students are uncomfortable with praise, because they just don't hear enough of it. It's an awkward feeling to see something positive about themselves displayed for all to see. That's okay. Let each deal with it in his own best way.

Say to your students, "I see that you've noticed the new display with everyone's name on it. I wrote one positive trait about each of you. I could have written many, but, for the sake of space, I only wrote one. Last night, I asked you to go home and think of one good quality you possess. Notice that there is a second blank next to each of your names. Before you leave today, I'd like for each of you to fill in that blank with that one positive quality. If you can fit two or three into the blank, that's fine, but I'm only asking for one."

Now leave this displayed for the rest of the school year, and notice how many times students walk up to it and admire it.

Notice the good inside of me
And then you'll also help me to see
That I have possibility
So tell me I'm good, and better I'll be!

Think About It

If you want to know what a student wants and needs from you, his teacher, ask him! We interviewed students from Kindergarten through twelfth grade and asked them what their ideal teacher would be like. Not surprisingly, their answers were remarkably similar. Here is a summary of what students told us they want and need from their teachers:

♦ To be nice and smile often
♦ To care about them
♦ To be understanding and patient
♦ To help them when they are struggling
♦ To be fair and consistent
♦ To enjoy teaching
♦ To be trustworthy
♦ To get to know them
♦ To believe in them
♦ To speak calmly to them
♦ To make learning interesting and fun
♦ To not embarrass them in front of their peers
♦ To challenge them to be their best
♦ To help them succeed
♦ To never give up on them

The list goes on, but you get the point. It is surprising to find that many teachers never ask their students what they want, need, and expect to gain from the class and from their teacher.

Do It

If you ask your students what they want and need from you, you're sure to hear the same things listed above. But ask them anyway, as the fact that you ask says you care about them and listen to them.

Done!

Though you cannot possibly accommodate every student's every want and need, you can definitely be the kind of teacher described in the previous list. Every child deserves to have that teacher every year!

---

[10]Breaux and Whitaker, *Seven Simple Secrets*, 2006. Larchmont, NY: Eye On Education.

Yesterday, we established what most, if not all, students want and need from their teachers. Hopefully, you have allowed your own students to tell you what they want and need from you. Take that list (or ours from yesterday) and turn it into your own Teacher's Creed that you proudly display in your classroom. It might look like this:

My Promises to You, My Students

I promise to be nice and smile often.
I promise to care about each of you.
I promise to be understanding.
I promise to help you when you are struggling.
I promise to be patient with you.
I promise to be fair and consistent.
I promise to enjoy teaching you.
I promise to be trustworthy.
I promise never to scream at you.
I promise that I will get to know you.
I promise to believe in you.
I promise to make learning interesting and meaningful.
I promise that I will not embarrass you in front of your peers.
I promise that I will challenge you to be your very best.
I promise to do everything I can to help you succeed.
And I promise that, no matter what, I will never give up on you.

And, by the way, if you ever apply for a teaching position at another school, show this to the administrator during your interview. These are the kinds of teachers that administrators LOVE to hire, because anyone who can proudly display this in his or her room and be committed to being this kind of teacher is a rare gem—that special teacher that every student deserves!

---

[11]Breaux and Whitaker, *Seven Simple Secrets*, 2006. Larchmont, NY: Eye On Education.

Think About It

Consider the following scenario:

> Nicole is not doing her work. You calmly say to her, "I need for you to get busy." Nicole, in an angry outburst, says, "I'm not doing anything, you _____ !" (We're certain you can fill in the blank.)

Question: When Nicole says this to you, where do all eyes in the classroom go—on Nicole or on YOU? You guessed it—they go on you. "How will the teacher react?" is the question in the mind of every student in the class, including Nicole. So what do you do? First, we'll suggest what NOT to do. Please don't do what many teachers do by reacting and asking something like, "What did you just say?" in an angry tone. Do you really want to hear what she said twice? Of course you don't. The danger in reacting too quickly is that you will say something that is inappropriate and unprofessional. And you can't take it back.

Do It

The technique we are about to share works with a situation like we just described and with almost any situation where a student loses control.

First, know, in advance, that any time a student loses control, you want to appear calm and in control, whether you feel that way or not. Say to Nicole, calmly, "I can see you're really upset right now. I'll speak with you when you calm down." And then smile at everyone else and start teaching like it's the happiest day of your life. Later, simply take Nicole aside, privately, and say, "Nicole, what happened? I felt so bad for you when you lost it in class. What's wrong?" She may or may not share what is wrong. So listen. Then say, "I'm not going to tell you that what you did was inappropriate because I know you know that. But if you ever feel that amount of frustration building again, give me a signal, and I'll get you out of the room so you don't embarrass yourself in front of all your friends. Now let's go back to class."

Done!

There was no power struggle. The students are stunned. Nicole is confused.

You may have a few questions regarding our technique. Tomorrow, we'll analyze the situation and tell you why the technique we shared works.

Think About It

Yesterday, we shared the scenario where Nicole lost her cool—and you were the unlucky recipient of her wrath. How fortunate for her, however, that she was in YOUR class when it happened and not in the classroom of a less effective teacher who engages in power struggles with students.

Do It

After reading the technique we shared, you may have a few questions. We'll attempt to anticipate and answer them. First, no one can argue that there was no power struggle because you appeared calm and in control. By not arguing back, you took all the power away from her. Your students were amazed at your professionalism because, quite frankly, this is not the type of reaction that is "typical" from some of their teachers. Then, you dealt with Nicole privately, so no one knows what really happened except you and Nicole. You may be wondering, "But what will the students say if Nicole tells them all I did was talk to her?" Some students will probably ask Nicole, "What happened?" The good news is that Nicole will give the same one-word answer that all students give when asked that question: "Nothing." Students always say that. No one believes them. They don't even believe each other. Therefore, no worries there.

But what about the fact that you didn't punish Nicole? With our technique, there is no punishment. But we're not going to tell you that you should or should not punish her. That is up to you. However, you accomplished what you wanted to accomplish—the student was not engaged in a struggle with the teacher, the teacher put the responsibility on the student as opposed to acting personally offended and daring the student to do it again, and the teacher appeared in control at all times. When you accomplish this with a student, the student is much less likely to repeat the behavior. That's really what teachers want—to eliminate the behavior and help to ensure that it doesn't happen again.

One more point: You said to Nicole, "I'm not going to tell you that what you did was inappropriate because I know you know that." See Day 158 for more on that technique.

Done!

The more out of control a student gets, the more IN CONTROL you must become!

DAY 154

Think About It

Do you remember taking courses in college on the subject of dealing with student behavior problems? We all attended those. And they're important. As teachers, we often need to use the skill of analyzing misbehavior, determining its cause, and then pulling from our bag of tricks to treat its symptoms. We hope that the techniques we use will help to deter a repeat of the misbehavior.

Now do you remember taking courses in college on the subject of analyzing GOOD behavior, determining its causes and then using that knowledge to help maximize it on a daily basis? To the best of our knowledge, that course is not offered.

If you know what causes good behavior, you can continue to foster it in your classroom, lessening the likelihood of bad behavior. We continue to learn why great teachers deal with fewer discipline problems than less effective teachers.

Do It

We'll give you a mini-course on almost everything you need to know about analyzing and maximizing good behavior. Here it is, in a nutshell:

- When students are engaged in meaningful activities, there is very little time for misbehavior.
- When teachers appear organized, prepared, happy, enthusiastic, and approachable, student behavior improves tremendously.
- When students feel successful, they behave better and try harder.
- Teachers who enjoy positive rapport with students experience fewer behavior problems in their classrooms.
- Teachers who have specific classroom management plans and implement those plans consistently enjoy better student behavior.
- Teachers who hide their buttons from their students and don't engage in power struggles have very few classroom discipline problems.

If you're doing all these things, you are experiencing much fewer discipline problems than a teacher who is not. If you're not doing these, you're struggling.

Done!

Students will always be tempted to misbehave. But knowing what causes GOOD behavior and using that knowledge to foster even better behavior are two of the most essential skills you can possess.

DAY 156

Think About It

We've all been guilty of it. . . . We start out with the best of intentions, but the follow-through is weak. We develop a classroom management plan, but we don't always implement it consistently. We tell students they must raise their hands for permission to speak, but then we answer a student's question even if he didn't raise his hand. One student notices that, so he does the same. Soon, lots of students are talking, and we become upset. But whose fault is it that the situation got out of hand? Ours. We simply forgot to be consistent. Students spot our inconsistent ways and do what human nature tells them to do—see how much they can get away with! We organize our classrooms and vow that we will remain organized, but soon we are enveloped in disorganization. We set aside time, every day, to work on planning and grading. Before we know it, we're using that time to do other things, and those other things are usually not even necessary. Regardless, we've now fallen behind on our paperwork and we're mad at ourselves because we told ourselves we would not procrastinate this year!

Things don't usually fall apart all at once. They fall apart gradually, as we become less and less persistent in being consistent.

Do It

It's no surprise that great teachers are better than the rest at being consistent. They tell students what they expect, and they continue to expect those things all year long. They are consistently organized. They consistently stay on top of their work loads. They consistently work at being consistent! They are consistently professional.

How consistent are you—in planning, in managing, in teaching, in dealing with student behavior issues, and in acting professionally? Decide which, if any, of those areas need improvement, and work at becoming more consistent.

Done!

When teachers are persistent in being consistent, discipline problems are almost nonexistent.
And teach they do, reaching me, reaching you—to that, no one is resistant!

Chaotic or Melodic?

Think About It

Myth: A quiet classroom is a symbol of an effective classroom.

We know of some teachers who pride themselves on the fact that you can walk past their classrooms on any day, at any time and hear a pin drop. They don't realize that, though there are definitely times when a quiet classroom is appropriate—such as when students are taking a test or are involved in an independent assignment—classrooms are supposed to be humming with learning!

Other teachers would agree with us about the fact that classrooms should be abuzz with activity, yet they fear that someone may walk by and think that students are simply having fun and not learning. Here's the good news: Anyone can tell the difference between structured noise and chaos. The two do not sound remotely similar. If you walk past a classroom where management is lacking and students are just blurting out and talking to one another, you will immediately recognize that noise as chaos. You will hear the teacher warning and begging students to be quiet. You will hear lots of discontent, both from the students and the teacher. Chaos! But walk past a room where students are having a discussion about a concept or topic, or students are buzzing within their groups, and the noise is easily recognized as structured noise. Again, anyone can tell the difference between *structured noise* and *chaos*.

Do It

Assess the sounds in your classroom. Ask yourself the following questions: If someone walked past my door, what would they typically hear? Would they hear laughter and learning? Would they hear spirited debates and meaningful discussions? Would they sometimes hear students answering teacher questions in unison? Would they hear groups working together to solve problems? If so, then as long as the noise does not disturb nearby classrooms, it's GOOD noise! But if you determine that your classroom is usually a very quiet place, you may want to add some noise to it. Structured noise, that is.

Done!

Just because your classroom's not quiet
Does not mean that you'll be inciting a riot
For structured noise is the noise of learning
Where the gears of young minds are constantly turning!

Think About It

Believe it or not, one of the best ways to get a student to do something is to tell him that you're not going to tell him to do whatever it is you actually want him to do! A little psychology can go a long way.

Do It

Before we give you examples, we want to point out that the only way this technique will be effective is if you appear calm and professional. If you appear bent out of shape and aggravated with the student, the technique simply doesn't work. In fact, when you are out of control and unprofessional, no technique works!

Try these and prepare to be amazed:

♦ I'm not going to tell you to sit, because I know you're on your way back to your desk. Thanks.
♦ I'm not going to tell you not to talk on the way to lunch, because I know you know we don't want to disturb anyone. Thanks.
♦ I'm not going to tell you to stop that, because I know you know it's inappropriate. Thanks.
♦ I'm not going to tell you that this isn't your best effort, because I know you already know that and that you'll give it your best next time. Thanks.
♦ I'm not going to tell you that that was a bad choice you made, because I know you already know that. And I know you'll make a better choice next time. Thanks.
♦ I'm not going to tell you to apologize to her for those hurtful words, because I know you were going to do that anyway. Thanks.
♦ I'm not going to tell you to get busy, because I can tell you're about to get started. Thanks.

Done!

By saying "I'm not going to tell you to behave"
Telling you to behave, I did
I am the adult, you see
My motive, from you, I hid
For sometimes adults have to trick kids into behaving
Whatever it takes, we're willing to do it, and all of our sanities we're saving!

Change the Scenery to Greenery

Think About It

Have you ever been cooped up for a while? Maybe in a hospital room? Or in your own house due to bad weather? What did it feel like when you finally got out and experienced a change in scenery? Even if the new scenery wasn't beautiful, didn't it feel good just to experience something different?

The same scenery, day in and day out, can sometimes make people lose interest or feel claustrophobic. Even the most beautiful scenery can lose its beauty if it's all you see. Have you ever found yourself obsessing about a problem, desperately trying to find a solution but feeling stuck inside your own thoughts, feeling as if you couldn't think straight, and then, when you WEREN'T thinking about it, the perfect solution just came to you? That's because you changed the scenery (your thoughts) in your head.

We all need a change of scenery from time to time. It's rejuvenating. And who of us couldn't use an occasional dose of rejuvenation?

Do It

Even if your classroom is a beautiful place, replete with color and comfort and all things cheerful, same-old, same-old can become lame-old (see Day 169). Plan to take your students outside every now and then and conduct a lesson there. Students of all ages LOVE when their teachers do this. They're never too young or old to benefit from a change of scenery. Just be sure to establish, clearly, what you will expect of them when the scenery changes. Don't make the mistake of taking them outside and THEN trying to explain to them how you expect them to behave. Also, tell them that if you see that they behave well and respond well to having class outside, you may just do it again soon.

Done!

WARNING: Changing your classroom scenery to greenery every once in a while May cause your students to be more engaged, to accomplish more, and to smile!

DAY 159

20-Day Reality Check

Following is a simple survey for you to complete based on all topics we have discussed since the previous 20-Day Reality Check. Your assignment today is simply to complete the survey. For each statement, write "Yes" or "No" in the right-hand column.

Survey

1	I incorporate games into my teaching.	
2	I occasionally reward my students with unexpected treats.	
3	I have gotten a coworker to stop by and tell my students that I have been singing their praises.	
4	I realize that teaching can be stressful, and I use techniques to keep my stress level under control.	
5	I have answered the questions from Day 147 regarding how my students would describe me.	
6	I have begun sending "I'm Proud of Your Child" notes to parents.	
7	I have used the "Good, Understood" suggestion from Days 149 and 150.	
8	I have devised and displayed my own "Teacher's Creed."	
9	I realize that the more *out of control* a student becomes, the more *in control* I must be.	
10	I am learning to analyze and maximize good behavior.	
11	I am becoming more consistent with my students and with my work habits.	
12	My classroom often hums with structured noise.	
13	I have attempted the "I'm Not Going to Tell You" technique.	
14	I have taken my students outside for a lesson in order to change the scenery.	

What I Learned/What I'll Do Differently

Based on yesterday's survey results, take a few minutes to list what you have learned, what you may have already known but needed to be reminded of, what you've noticed about your students, what you will attempt to do differently in your teaching from this point forward.

_____

_____

_____

_____

_____

_____

_____

_____

_____

_____

_____

_____

_____

_____

_____

_____

_____

_____

_____

_____

_____

_____

_____

_____

_____

_____

_____

DAY 161

DAY 162

Think About It

We often hear it said that *attitude is everything.* We often tell students that their attitudes need to improve. But do we ever actually teach them WHY attitude is so important and provide them with tools for understanding and improving their attitudes? Nagging a person about his poor attitude will ensure one thing—a poorer attitude. But arming a person with tools, tricks, and techniques for improving his attitude can actually make it fun for that person to work on improving his attitude. And we all know that students like to have fun and like to feel successful.

For the next five days, we will walk you through simple steps you can take to help your students improve their attitudes. Even students with great attitudes can still improve their attitudes, so this activity will benefit everyone, including you.

Do It

Hold a brief discussion with students about attitude—its definition, its importance to success in life, its importance in relationships with others, and the fact that attitudes are actually contagious. Talk about your own attitude, sharing what you do continually to improve it. Discuss the fact that people with good attitudes tend to be happier people, have more friends, experience more success in life, and have positive impacts on the people around them. Tell them that the entire class, including you, will be playing an "attitude game" for the next five days. And tell them that on the fifth day, anyone whose attitude has shown improvement will receive a prize. (You'll have to determine what that prize will be.) Now you've got their attention! Students of all ages love prizes.

Their simple assignment today will be to list five traits of people they know whom they consider to have great attitudes. That's it. You'll collect these from them tomorrow. (Note that for very young students, you may wish to have them simply tell you about someone they know who is very positive.)

Done!

By helping students' attitudes to improve
Their negative behavior, you help them to remove!

Think About It

Yesterday, you had students list five traits of people with positive attitudes. You'll collect those today, but there's really no need to go over all of them. You simply wanted to get your students thinking about what kinds of traits people with positive attitudes possess.

Today, we'd like to focus on one trait in particular that people with positive attitudes possess—the ability to take a failure or a negative situation or a bad day and turn it into a positive learning experience. Henry Ford said, "Failure is only the opportunity to begin again more intelligently." Now that's a great attitude! Imagine what your students could and would accomplish in your classroom (and in life) if they possessed this kind of attitude.

Do It

For today's activity, share the Henry Ford quote (or a similar one) with your students. Discuss it briefly, and have a few students share with you ways in which they have turned negative situations into positive learning experiences. Tell them their attitude challenge today is to take one negative situation, be it at home or at school, and turn it into a positive learning experience. For instance, if a student gets a poor test grade, maybe he can use the information on the test to help him to see what he did wrong and correct it or ask questions of you if he does not understand. If a student upsets someone at home or at school by saying something he should not have said, maybe he can use this opportunity to apologize for his actions and heal the relationship. If a student is struggling with improving at a particular sport and is becoming frustrated with his progress, maybe he can see this as an opportunity to analyze what he's doing incorrectly and practice on improving rather than giving up. If you put students into groups and a student does not like someone in his group, maybe he can decide to have a positive attitude about it and refrain from complaining. These are just a few examples you may want to share with your students in order to help them come up with ways of turning negative situations into positive learning opportunities.

Done!

If you can help students to become aware of the importance of possessing a positive attitude, that is a huge accomplishment! It will affect the way they behave and the way they achieve. Time well spent!

DAY 163

DAY 164

Think About It

One saw a glass half empty
The other, a glass half full
What? It was the same glass?
What stunt were they trying to pull?
No stunt was pulled at all, you see
Our attitudes shape our vision
We all get to choose for ourselves
Whether life's an adventure or a collision!

Do It

Share this poem with your students. Take only about two minutes to review what you have discussed over the last few days regarding positive attitudes, and then give your students a simple assignment that they may choose to complete either at home or at school. The assignment is as follows: Tell students to take a problem they are having and to come up with one idea for a positive solution to the problem. Remind them that even if their idea for a solution does not work, they have at least learned one thing that doesn't work. Now they can try something else. The key is to help them learn not to get bogged down in the fear or frustration of failure, but to continue to search for new ways to solve problems.

Remind them about the prize they will receive in two days when they can show how their attitudes have improved. Also, by now, you may be noticing a few students displaying more positive attitudes. Point this out to them so that they know that you are noticing the improvement.

Done!

Tell students to write just a sentence or two about their results from today's assignment, and let them know you will collect these tomorrow.

Think About It

On Day 97, we spoke about the importance of wearing a smile. We talked about the fact that when you smile, your brain releases endorphins which are your body's natural pain killers. So, when you smile, you immediately begin to feel better. We encouraged you to smile often in the classroom. Today, we'd like for you to share this information with your students.

Do It

Take a few minutes to tell students what happens in the brain when a person smiles. Then prove it to them. Have them all think of something that is upsetting to them—something that makes them sad, mad, depressed. Assure them you will not ask them to share it with anyone. As they do this, you will notice that facial expressions change, eyes look downward, and so on. Then say, "Now I'd like everyone to start smiling. Smile the biggest smile you can possibly smile. Keep smiling and try to feel upset again. Keep smiling. Think about what's upsetting you, but keep smiling. Don't stop smiling, but get back to that feeling of being upset." Guess what! They can't. You can't feel upset when you are smiling.

Point? You can literally change your attitude by smiling! You have just given them a tool to use in order to improve their attitudes. No, you are not suggesting to them that all of life's problems can be solved by simply smiling. But attitudes can "improve" by smiling, and that's what you're going for here. Students love this activity. Try it.

Done!

Collect yesterday's assignment. If a student has *forgotten* his at home, say, "That's okay. It was just a sentence or two, so rewrite it and give it to me before you leave." Remind them that tomorrow there will be prizes awarded for improved attitudes.

DAY 165

Think About It

For the past few days, you have been helping students to work on improving their attitudes. Please remember that ANY improvement is a good thing! The better a student's attitude, the more likely he is to behave and learn. The more tools he has for improving his own attitude, the better will be the chances that he actually works at improving his attitude. The bottom line is that all teachers want to teach students who have good attitudes, so taking time to help them learn to improve their attitudes is time well spent!

Do It

Whatever your prize today consists of, be it a sticker or a snack or a pass that allows them to skip an assignment—here is how each student will win that prize: Tell students to write either a few sentences or a list describing what they have done to improve their attitudes over the last few days. (If you have the time, you might even allow them to share these with the class.) As you collect this from each student, he receives his prize. As you give him his prize, praise him for his efforts. That's it!

Make an effort to continue to notice improvements in attitudes and to continue to encourage students to improve their attitudes. We can all use a little *attitude adjustment* from time to time. Continue to remind yourself, also, that your attitude helps to set the tone in your classroom each day.

Done!

Praise your students for attitude improvement, and attitude improvement you'll see! Nag them about bad attitudes they possess, and bad attitude possessors they'll be.

DAY 166

Be a Guide on the Side

Think About It

Teachers are often told to be a *guide on the side* as opposed to a *sage on the stage*. When we think of a *sage on the stage*, we think about someone merely professing knowledge. This is not to say that a teacher should never profess knowledge. It IS to say, however, that we feel teachers should be in the *guide* role more so than in the *professor* mode. To illustrate our point, we liken great teachers to great coaches. Great coaches do a little professing and a LOT of guiding from the sidelines. They never take their eyes off of their players. They continually monitor, encourage, motivate, teach and reteach, cheer, change the game plan to meet the needs of the players, and use everything they observe to help them continue to coach their players and help their players improve. It's really no different from great teaching. The arenas may look different, but great teaching is great coaching and vice versa. In the hands of a great coach, the players are actively involved most of the time. In the hands of a great teacher, the students are actively involved most of the time.

Do It

Consider yourself a coach in the classroom, teaching, training, motivating, instructing, and guiding your players (students) constantly, leading them in discussions and helping them to solve problems in order to improve their performance. With this type of teaching (coaching) in the classroom, there is very little time where the teacher is lecturing and the students' only involvement is listening. Coaching them involves providing ongoing feedback in order to help move them forward, pushing them to new heights. Students are actively engaged most of the time. They also learn to work individually and cooperatively when they become a part of a team.

For today's activity, simply monitor your teaching. How much time are you spending lecturing while the students are passively engaged? How much time are you actually serving as a guide, a coach, on the sidelines? What could you do differently to move more toward being a coach in the classroom?

Done!

Show me how and let me do it, and stay right beside me as you guide me through it
And cheer for me and tell me how I'm doing, and a smarter ME, I will be pursuing!

DAY 168

Think About It

A principal, his best teacher, and his secretary stumbled upon a bottle on their way to lunch. They picked it up and a genie appeared, granting them each one wish. The teacher said, "I want to be on a cruise ship sailing to all the islands of Hawaii." Poof! She was gone. The secretary said, "I want to be on my own private island, relaxing on my own private beach having nothing to do and no one around." Poof! She was gone. The principal said, "I want those two back right after lunch!"

Do It

Have you heard any good jokes lately—good, clean, fun jokes or riddles or puns that you would feel comfortable sharing with your students? Students love to laugh, and they will even laugh at corny jokes. Even if they pretend that what you said is not in the least bit funny, don't be deterred. Students love teachers who joke with them.

Especially as the school year nears its close, it's too easy to get too serious. Sometimes we need to remind ourselves to lighten up and have fun with our students. And an easy way to have fun with your students is to share an occasional joke with them. So share a joke with your students today. If you don't have any, ask a coworker or go online to one of many sites providing lots of good, clean jokes for teachers and students.

Done!

Teacher: You missed school yesterday, didn't you?
Student: Not very much.

Mother: Why does your test paper have a big zero on it?
Child: It's not a zero. The teacher ran out of stars, so she gave me a moon instead!

Laughter is truly the best medicine. Laugh with yourself, at yourself, and with your students every day.

Same Can Be Lame

Think About It

Ever feel like you're stuck in a rut? Like you do the same thing, day in and day out, and that same thing has become a lame thing? At one time or another, we all feel that way. We get bored with our daily routine.

Even a game can soon become lame if it's always the same. Have you ever watched a football game that just went back and forth with no scoring and no excitement? The crowd becomes almost silent and many people in the stands (and we're talking about the ones who love football) lose interest and become bored. Then, out of nowhere, the ball is intercepted or there is a fumble and the crowd jumps up and begins cheering and, suddenly, everyone is once again attentive. The players suddenly begin playing with more fire and enthusiasm because they are now rejuvenated!

It's no different in the classroom. Even very effective teaching methods and engaging activities can become lame if they are always the same. On Day 159, we talked about changing the scenery to greenery by occasionally taking your students outside for a lesson. Today, we will talk about changing the scenery inside of your classroom, not by rearranging furniture or changing decorations, but by making a change in the way you teach.

Do It

Today's activity is simple. Talk to a colleague and get a new idea for teaching something you have always taught the same way. Then teach the same thing you have always taught, but in a different way.

Maybe instead of leading a classroom discussion, you'll let two students lead it. Maybe you'll learn a different way to introduce a concept. Maybe you'll simply change the order of things you typically do in class. Maybe you'll allow students to create their own games to review for a test. Just as a sudden turnover in a football game can invigorate both the fans and the players, a turnover in the way you teach can invigorate both your students and you!

Done!

Of life, variety is the spice
Which is why a change can feel so nice
So the more variety you have in your teaching
The more your students you will be reaching!

Avoid Being Statuesque at Your Desk[12]

Think About It

There's something called a teacher's desk
And its purpose is for storage
It holds your stuff so that when you need something
You know just where to forage.

In almost every classroom, there is a piece of furniture known as a teacher's desk. It actually has two purposes: (1) to store stuff and (2) to sit at when students are not in the room. There are no other purposes for that piece of furniture. But some teachers have never received that memo, and they actually sit at their desks when the students are in the room. That's a huge mistake. Here's why: A physical barrier creates a mental barrier. It separates people physically, thus emotionally separating them also. The last thing you want is to be emotionally separated from your students. You want them to know that you are just like a coach, right in the game with them. (Please notice that there is never a coach's desk on the sideline of a football field.)

Do It

Feel free to sit at your desk any time the students are not present. But when the students are present, even when they are working independently, it is vital that you are *in the game* with them. As we've already discussed (see Day 113), the farther you are from a student, the more likely he is to misbehave. If, for some reason, you must occasionally sit while teaching, simply take your chair from behind your desk and put it right in the center of your students.

Done!

You're not a judge in a courtroom, on a raised platform behind the "bench"
But rather you're a teacher of thirsty students whose thirst is yours to quench
Students should not need permission to approach
Or be warned that on your space they must not encroach
For you're not a judge in a courtroom. You're a teacher, the ultimate coach
The person who, more than any other, is completely safe to approach!

---

[12]Breaux, *101 "Answers" for New Teachers and Their Mentors* (2nd ed.), 2011. Larchmont, NY: Eye On Education.

Think About It

Teaching is not easy. It never was and never will be. If you're doing it well, you're working hard. So sometimes it's tempting to give in to the feelings of being overwhelmed and simply take the easy way out.

Let's face it:

◆ The old lecture, read the chapter, and answer the questions at the end of the chapter method is easy, but it's not what's best for your students.
◆ Assigning worksheets 25 to 28 is easier than engaging them in activities where they discuss, explore, and interact, but it's not what's best for your students.
◆ Objective tests are much easier to grade than are more authentic types of assessment, but they're not always what's best for your students.
◆ Teaching all students as if they were at one level is easier than teaching at varying levels, but it's not what's best for your students.
◆ Maintaining your composure and professionalism at all times is not always easy, but it is ALWAYS what's best for your students.

Do It

Every day, you make many decisions—in your planning, in your management, and in your teaching. And many times, you second guess yourself before or after making a decision. That's because you're a professional, and true professionals are always harder on themselves than are their less professional counterparts.

Here is a simple way never to second guess yourself again. Before making any decision in your classroom, be it a simple one or a difficult one, ask yourself the following question:

Am I making the decision based on what's best for my students or am I making the decision based on what's easiest for me?

If you choose to make all decisions based on what's best for your students, you will be making good decisions.

Done!

Choose what's best for your students, and never what's easiest for you
For nothing worthwhile, such as reaching a child, will ever be easy to do!

Forgive and Forget

Think About It

If you've ever been hurt by someone, it's not always easy to forgive, and it's sometimes impossible to forget. That's true of adults, but not of children. Children are so innocent and so willing to forgive. They are even capable of forgetting, if you apologize, sincerely, for what you have done to hurt them. You want to set nothing but good examples for the students in your care. But if you set a bad example by saying something hurtful to a child, what better way to make amends and in turn set a good example than by owning your actions and apologizing!

Do It

To say, "I'm sorry, but . . ." and then tell the child that something HE did provoked what YOU did is ineffective. It comes across as insincere every time.

If you say or do something to hurt a child's feelings, try one of the following:

♦ I want to apologize for what I said to you. I know that was hurtful, and I should not have said that. I know how upset I would feel if someone had said that to me. I hope you can forgive me.
♦ I'm so sorry that I hurt your feelings. It was wrong of me to say what I said, and I'm truly sorry for saying it. I won't do it again. I hope you can forgive me.
♦ I'm truly sorry that I embarrassed you in front of your friends. That was insensitive on my part, and I can understand how that must have hurt you. I hope you can forgive me.

Own your actions, apologize for them, and children will almost always say the same two words: "That's okay." Not only will they say those words, but they'll actually forgive you. And not only will they forgive you, but they'll learn from the good example you set by apologizing.

Done!

Teacher, you spoke some words to me that hurt me to the core
And suddenly I really did not like you anymore
But then you said, "I'm sorry. I was wrong for what I said."
And so I said, "That's okay; I'll erase it from my head."
We're better on the inside than we sometimes act overtly
So I believe you when you tell me that you did not mean to hurt me
So thanks for the apology. I'll forgive and I'll forget
And now I owe my thanks to you for the good example you set.

DAY 172

Don't Overlook the Best for the Sake of the Rest

Think About It

They're in every class—the students who just cause no trouble at all. They're agreeable, they work hard, they make good grades, and, yes, they sometimes fade into the woodwork. Because we never have to worry about them, we often neglect them. They, above all students, deserve the most recognition and praise. But they don't demand it, so we sometimes just forget to give it. Neglecting to show our appreciation to these students is often one of our biggest mistakes. We assume that these students know how much we appreciate them, but they never will if we don't tell them.

Do It

Who are your very best students? You know, the ones you never have to reprimand, the ones who never cause you to lose sleep, the ones who make teaching almost easy. Write their names here:

_____

_____

_____

_____

_____

Whether you wrote the names of one or 20 students, make it a point today—don't wait another minute—to speak privately with each of them. And tell them, in no uncertain terms, just how much you appreciate their work ethic and good behavior. Let them know that they are special, and that none of their hard work has gone unnoticed. Let them know you will never forget them. Express your gratitude to them, your belief in them, and your apologies for not thanking them enough. You can never thank these kinds of students enough. You may even want to write a note home saying the same things to their parents.

Done!

The student who does everything right can sometimes go undetected
He's the one who, by you, teacher, can be unintentionally neglected
So take the time to let him know you appreciate all he does
Not to do so just may be the biggest mistake there ever was.

Think About It

The end of the school year is almost here, and for weeks and months, I shall disappear!

Since the end of the year is near, we share this tip for you to consider using next school year. People love quotes, because they amuse, inspire, entertain, or provoke deep thought. There are many books on the market filled with famous quotes. The Internet is replete with great quotes also.

Here's one of our favorites: "What sculpture is to a block of marble, education is to the soul" (Joseph Addison).

Do It

Students also love quotes. Teachers often use them for the reasons we listed above—to amuse, inspire, entertain, or provoke deep thought. We encourage you to try what a fellow teacher shared with us:

> I have a quote board. Every day, I change the quote. On some days, the quote relates to a concept we are learning. Other times, the quote provokes thought in my students. Some quotes are put there just to make them laugh. Sometimes we discuss the quote in class, but even on days when I don't have time for a discussion, the quote is always there for all to see. I put students in charge of changing the quote each day. Students love having this job in my class, and it's a job they never forget to do. About midyear, I allow the students to start writing their own quotes for the board. I've been amazed at their creativity and their wisdom.

You might also have students bring in their favorite quotes so you can add them to your stockpile. Also, many people post daily quotes on Twitter, Facebook, and other social media websites. Feel free to "borrow" from them.

Done!

"Education is the best provision for old age" (Aristotle). May all of our students live long, happy, successful, educated lives!

Orange You Glad?

Think About It

We attended a conference and listened to the keynote speaker addressing a room full of thousands of teachers. He held up an orange and asked, "If I squeeze this orange, what will come out of it?" The teachers responded, "Juice." "What kind of juice?" asked the speaker. "Orange juice," replied the teachers. "Why not lemon juice?" asked the speaker. "Because it's an orange and not a lemon," replied the teachers. "Oh, so you're saying that you can only get out of something what's already inside of it?" asked the speaker. "Yes," replied the teachers.

Do you see where he was going with this? He went on to say that when you push a person's buttons, you can only get out of that person what is already in that person. Nothing else. Just what's already inside. If you take a positive teacher and put her in the presence of negative students, nothing but a positive attitude and professionalism will come out of her, no matter how hard the students push. Sadly, the reverse is also true. "Have you ever met a teacher who insisted that the students were driving her crazy?" he asked. The teachers laughed and nodded. "Well," he said, "crazy has already got to be in there!"

The fact is that you cannot get out of someone what is not already inside of that person. Are you an orange or are you a lemon?

Do It

We have taken this activity and used it both with teachers and students. Try it with your students. Then explain to them that who they are on the inside will always reveal itself through their actions. Discuss the fact that their friends can't make them do anything. We all have to decide whether we're oranges or lemons, sweet or sour.

And never forget that you get to choose, regardless of your circumstances, how you react in any situation.

Done!

Be an orange as opposed to a lemon
One who's always praisin', not complainin' and condemnin'.

Think About It

On Day 93, we recommended that you have an awards ceremony for your students. If you did, then this will be Part 2. If not, then give it a try this time. Make sure that every student leaves your class this year having won some type of award. Remember that the awards do not need to be elaborate or expensive. They simply need to signify recognition for a job well done.

Do It

As a refresher from Day 93, plan a very simple awards ceremony for your entire class. You can either print the awards on your computer or make them by hand. The key is to present every student with some type of award during your ceremony. Here are a few ideas for awards: most improved, best behavior, most helpful, best attendance record, most kind, most likely to _____ (you can fill in that blank with endless possibilities), most creative, funniest, best grade point average, best attitude.

The ceremony will take only a few minutes, but it will be more than worth your time and effort. It will also show your students that you noticed, this year, something good in each of them.

Done!

Present every student in your class with some type of award
An award for being the most improved, an award for trying hard
An award to say that you have noticed something each achieved
An award that lets each student know that in them you believed.

A Letter for You

All year long, we have talked about how important it is that your students know you believe in them. We cannot think of a better, easier way to do that than the following:

Write a simple letter (or use ours) and give it to each of your students. Tell them to keep this letter and to return it to you some day. As you will see, the letter expresses your belief that each will become successful. You don't really even need to give the students your address. It would be great if, one day, you would receive a few of these letters from former students. But the real purpose of this activity is to express belief in them.

Here's a sample letter:

Dear Mrs./Mr. _____ :
(your name)

I just wanted you to know that I am now a very successful _____
_____ .

A few things you might like to hear about me are _____
_____
_____
_____ .

I knew you would be proud of me. I am also very proud of myself.

Sincerely:

_____

When you give your students this letter, say to them, "I know you are all going to be very successful in life. I'm giving you this letter, and one day I want you to mail it back to me. I'll be so happy to hear of all the successes in life that I know you will enjoy."

The Goal Post Revisited

Think About It

On Day 88, we suggested that if you were to walk into almost any classroom and ask the students, "Who among you has written goals telling what you want to accomplish this year, next year, or further into your future?," you will see very few, if any, raised hands. We also shared an astounding study that proved the importance of having written goals.

On Days 88 through 91, you helped your students to create goals and you then allowed them to share those with the class. Now, before the end of the year, you have an opportunity to encourage them to continue to set goals and to work toward achieving those goals.

Do It

Help your students to revisit their goals today, especially since it is the end of the school year. Here's a simple step-by-step plan for doing that:

1. Remind your students about the importance of having written goals.
2. Have them think about the goals they set for themselves earlier in the school year.
3. Ask them to share any progress they have made toward their goals.
4. Remind them to aim high when goal setting.
5. Express your belief that they can achieve their goals.
6. Remind them not to be put off by failures as they work toward achieving their goals.

Done!

By helping your students to understand the importance of positive goal setting and by having them write and now revisit those goals, you have put them among the tiny percentage of people who have written goals.

You've done your part, and you've done something that very few teachers do, regrettably. It's the little things that separate the great teachers from all the rest. Thanks for doing your part. The rest is up to them.

The Final Word That Everyone Heard

On Day 1, we talked about the importance of first impressions. Today, we'll talk about the importance of last impressions. Both first and last impressions are lasting. Never forget that you are carried in the hearts of every student you have ever taught—for the rest of their lives. Knowing that, you will want to leave them this year with a positive last impression.

On your very last day with them, be sure to do the following:

♦ Thank your students for spending this year with you.
♦ Tell your students it has been a privilege to teach them this year.
♦ Tell them you hope that they have come to realize that every decision you made this year was made with their best interests at heart.
♦ Express belief in each of them.
♦ Remind them of some of their accomplishments in your class this year.
♦ Reminisce about a few funny things that happened this year, and tell them you will cherish these memories.
♦ Tell them you will miss them.
♦ Tell them that they are one of the most special groups of students you have ever taught. (Yes, say this to every class every year.)
♦ Wish them nothing but success in their futures.
♦ Tell them you have grown to care about each of them and that you will never forget them.

As they leave your class, thank each of them on their way out and wish them well. Make sure that the last expression they see on your face is a positive one. Give them your best and biggest smile!

DAY 179

Final 20-Day Reality Check

Here is this year's final survey. For each statement, write "Yes" or "No" in the right-hand column.

Survey

1	I have taken steps toward helping my students to improve their attitudes.	
2	I am aware that my attitude sets the daily tone in my classroom.	
3	I view myself as more of a *guide on the side* than a *sage on the stage*.	
4	I occasionally share jokes with my students.	
5	I am careful to add variety to my teaching.	
6	I avoid sitting at my desk while the students are present.	
7	I make decisions based on what is best for my students as opposed to what is easiest for me.	
8	I am careful to offer a sincere apology if I hurt a student's feelings or say something I should not have said.	
9	I have been careful not to overlook my best students.	
10	I am planning to implement the suggestion for "Quote of the Day/Week" next school year.	
11	I have used the "orange" technique from Day 175.	
12	I have held an awards ceremony for my students.	
13	I have used the "letter" suggestions from Day 177.	
14	I am leaving my students with positive words.	

For now, you've earned a much-needed break. Here's hoping we have helped you to have a wonderful school year. And here's to an even better one next year!

Conclusion

Over the past 180 days, we have attempted to provide you with ideas, tips, suggestions, and activities for improving your effectiveness in the classroom. Even if you've implemented only a few, you have taken steps toward improvement. If you were a good teacher before you picked this book up, we hope we have helped you to become a great teacher. If you were already a great teacher, then we hope you are now an even greater teacher.

No one ever finishes learning to teach. As teachers, we are on a never-ending quest for new and better ways to accomplish the one thing we set out to do when we chose this profession—positively affect lives. We hope we have helped you on your quest. We thank you for reading our book, we thank you for choosing to make a difference, and we wish you many years of continued success in the classroom.

> *Teacher, Did You Know?*
> *Teacher, did you know*
> *That you are a hero?*
> *You touch a heart, you teach a mind*
> *You heal a wound; what's lost, you find*
> *You motivate the unmotivated*
> *You simplify what's complicated*
> *You nurture all your flowers, removing all the weeds*
> *You're an ordinary person performing extraordinary deeds!*

An Invitation for Your Comments

As with all of our books, we eagerly invite your input, your suggestions, or any stories you may wish to share for our future writings. Please feel free to contact us at: **author@eyeoneducation.com**

Please include our names in the subject line.

All poetry in this book is the original work of Annette Breaux.

Notes for Next Year

We also recommend . . .

50 Ways to Improve Student Behavior:
Simple Solutions to Complex Challenges
Annette L. Breaux and Todd Whitaker

From best-selling authors Annette Breaux and Todd Whitaker, *50 Ways to Improve Student Behavior: Simple Solutions to Complex Challenges* is a must-read reference for teachers, both new and experienced!

In a lively and engaging style, Annette Breaux and Todd Whitaker share 50 simple, straightforward techniques for improving student behavior and increasing student cooperation, participation, and achievement. Each practical, well-defined strategy can be applied in classrooms of all grade levels and subjects. Strategies include:

♦ How to make students more responsible
♦ How to nip potential problems in the bud
♦ Learning what to overlook
♦ Establishing classroom rules and procedures
♦ Teaching in small bites (It makes students hungrier!)

As student behavior improves, so too will the quality of learning in your classroom. With this book, you can begin to introduce a host of new strategies into your teaching practice today!

2010, 144 pp. paperback 978-1-59667-132-4 $29.95 plus shipping and handling

What Great Teachers Do *Differently*:

17 Things That Matter Most
(Second Edition)

Todd Whitaker

"Todd Whitaker's generous use of examples provides something everyone can relate to. His writing style is very easy to read. It is like having a conversation with a fellow teacher on what is best for kids."

Sharon Weber, Elementary Principal
Punxsutawney Area School District
Punxsutawney, PA

In the second edition of this renowned book, you will find pearls of wisdom, heartfelt advice, and inspiration from one of the nation's leading authorities on staff motivation, teacher leadership, and principal effectiveness. With wit and understanding, Todd Whitaker describes the beliefs, behaviors, attitudes, and interactions of great teachers and explains what they do differently. New features include:

♦ Meaning what you say

♦ Focusing on students first

♦ Putting yourself in their position

2012, 144 pp. paperback 978-1-59667-199-7 $29.95 plus shipping and handling

101 "Answers" for New Teachers and Their Mentors:

Effective Teaching Tips for Daily Classroom Use
(Second Edition)

Annette L. Breaux

"There is no one I can recommend more highly than Annette Breaux."
Harry K. Wong, Author of
The First Days of School

The second edition of this bestselling title features brand new strategies plus illustrations!

Make sure your new teachers are ready for the realities of the classroom. Be confident that their mentors are focused and effective. Organized so new teachers can read it by themselves, this book can also be studied collaboratively with veteran teachers who have been selected to mentor them.

Addressing the questions and struggles of all new teachers—with simple solutions—this book:

♦ Generates instant impact on teacher effectiveness

♦ Promotes communication between new teachers and their mentors

♦ Offers strategies for any teacher looking to become more effective

Topics include:

♦ Classroom Management

♦ Discipline

♦ Relating Lessons to Real Life

♦ Encouraging Active Student Participation

♦ Planning

♦ Professionalism, Attitudes and Behaviors of Effective Teachers

2011 176 pp. paperback 978-1-59667-182-9 $29.95 plus shipping and handling

Seven Simple Secrets:

What the BEST Teachers Know and Do!

Annette Breaux and Todd Whitaker

"A wonderful book for new teachers and their mentors."
Sharon Weber, Principal
Bell Township Elementary School, PA

This book reveals—

♦ The Secret of Classroom Management
♦ The Secret of Instruction
♦ The Secret of Attitude
♦ The Secret of Professionalism
♦ The Secret of Effective Discipline
♦ The Secret of Motivation and Inspiration

Implementing these secrets will change your life, both in and out of the classroom. But most importantly, implementing these secrets will enhance the lives of every student you teach.

2006, 160 pp. paperback 1-59667-021-5 $29.95 plus shipping and handling

REAL Teachers, REAL Challenges, REAL Solutions:
25 Ways to Handle the Challenges of the Classroom Effectively
Annette and Elizabeth Breaux

"After reading this book, your teaching will never be
the same. It is a must read for all teachers."
Harry K. Wong, Author of
The First Days of School

For new teacher induction programs or high interest staff development workshops, this book helps new teachers—and experienced ones—find solutions to common classroom challenges. It shows teachers how to get students to do what you want them to do, deal with parents and difficult coworkers, and solve other common teaching challenges. It presents 25 real scenarios along with "What's Effective," "What's NOT Effective," and "Bottom Line" strategies for handling teacher challenges.

2004, 120 pp. paperback 1-930556-64-0 $24.95

101 Poems for Teachers

Annette L. Breaux

One of the most sought-after and dynamic speakers in education, Annette Breaux has inspired audiences of teachers and administrators across the country. She has incorporated each of her presentations with her heartwarming original poetry. This collection brings together 101 of Breaux's poems, from which teachers and school staff can draw continued motivation and enjoyment.

I Teach

I light a spark in a darkened soul
I warm the heart of one grown cold
I look beyond and see within
Behind the face, beneath the skin
I quench a thirst, I soothe a pain
I provide the food that will sustain
I touch, I love, I laugh, I cry
Whatever is needed, I supply
Yet more than I give, I gain from each
I am most richly blessed—I teach!
—*Annette Breaux*

2010, 208 pp. paperback 978-1-59667-146-1 $19.95 plus shipping and handling

Teaching Matters:
Motivating & Inspiring Yourself
Todd and Beth Whitaker

"This book makes you want to be the best teacher you can be."
Nancy Fahnstock
Godby High School
Tallahassee, Florida

Celebrate the teaching life! This book helps teachers:

- rekindle the excitement of the first day of school all year long
- approach every day in a "Thank God it is Monday" frame of mind
- not let negative people ruin your day
- fall in love with teaching all over again

Brief Contents

- Why You're Worth It
- Unexpected Happiness
- Could I Have a Refill Please? (Opportunities for Renewal)
- Celebrating Yourself
- Raise the Praise–Minimize the Criticize
- Making School Work for You

2002, 150 pp. paperback 1-930556-35-7 $24.95 plus shipping and handling

Great Quotes for Great Educators
Todd Whitaker and Dale Lumpa

Over 600 insightful, witty nuggets to motivate and inspire you . . . and everyone else at your school. Teachers—display these quotes in your classrooms! Administrators—insert them into your faculty memos and share them at staff meetings!

Why is this book unique?

♦ It includes over 100 original quotes from internationally acclaimed speaker and educator Todd Whitaker.

♦ It features real quotes from real students, which echo wit and wisdom for educators.

♦ Each quote has a direct connection to your life as an educator.

Examples of quotes in this book:

"Great teachers have high expectations for their students, but higher expectations for themselves."
Todd Whitaker

"We can never control a classroom until we control ourselves."
Todd Whitaker

2004, 208 pp. paperback 1-903556-82-9 $29.95 plus shipping and handling